Memoir of
a Cocoa Farmer's Daughter

EARLIER PUBLICATIONS BY THE AUTHOR

Journal Article

(1990) *with* P. I. Gomes, "The CNIRD Initiative: Mobilising the NGO Sector for Rural Transformation." *Caribbean Affairs* 3:2 (April–June)

Conference Papers

(1990) "Rural Development Re-defined in the Context of a National Land Reform Programme: The Case of Grenada 1980-83." Presented at the 15th Annual Conference of the Caribbean Studies Association on *The Caribbean in the Year 2000*

(1999) "Poverty Reduction and the Engineer – A Rural Community Development Perspective." Presented at the 13th Annual Technical Conference of the Association of Professional Engineers of Trinidad and Tobago (APETT) on *The Engineer in Caribbean Society*

Contribution

(2000) "NGO Networking: Ring around the Roses." In *Spitting in the Wind: Lessons in Empowerment from the Caribbean*, ed. Suzanne Francis Brown. Kingston: Ian Randle Publishers in association with the Commonwealth Foundation

Memoir of a Cocoa Farmer's Daughter

From Caribbean Rural Development Activist To Rural Entrepreneur

REGINA DUMAS

ARAWAK
publications
KINGSTON · JAMAICA

A r a w a k publications
Kingston • Jamaica

22 21 20 19 18   5 4 3 2 1

Credits

Chapters 1–7 & p.161: photos/images reproduced by courtesy of:

Regina Dumas (author)

pp.162-164: "Glimpses of Cuffie River Nature Retreat" – Photos/images reproduced by courtesy of copyright owners➤

Faraaz Abdool (photo ID#s 5,11,16,17)
Gerry Flemming (photo ID#s 3,7,9,10,12)
Roger Neckles (Cover images & ID#20)
Brigitte Noel (photo ID#s 6,8,18)
Steve Wooler (photo ID#s 1,2,4,13,14,15,19,21)

NATIONAL LIBRARY OF JAMAICA
CATALOGUING–IN–PUBLICATION DATA

Dumas, Regina
Memoir of a cocoa farmer's daughter : from Caribbean
rural development activist to rural entrepreneur /
Regina Dumas

p. ; cm
ISBN 978-976-95836-9-6 (print)
ISBN 978-976-8282-08-8 (ebook)

1. Dumas, Regina – 1945-
2. Trinidad and Tobago – Biography
3. Entrepreneurship   I. Title

920   - dc 23

Set in Iowan Old Style Bk BT 10.5/13pt
with Gabriola and Type Embellishments One LET

Printed in the United Kingdom

Dedication

For my parents, with love

And to rural dwellers — everywhere

❧ Contents

❦ Foreword

THIS MEMOIR IS A testament of our time! "Our time" refers to the experiences of those born in the Anglophone Caribbean in the 1940s and benefitting from the socio-economic and educational opening up of society enabled by political independence from colonial rule in the 1960s. Indeed, it is important to have testaments of various generations, to enable the voiceless to see their life trajectories in the light of the paths of others of their own vintage. Regina Dumas throws a refreshing light on her unfolding of social, intellectual, and spiritual consciousness, from a girlhood in Chaguanas and Tunapuna in Trinidad, to a travelled professional and mother of two, to a risk-taking entrepreneur in eco-tourism. The geographic range of her travels in her career with non-governmental organizations spans almost all the islands of the Caribbean, Switzerland, the Soviet Union, Malaysia, and Central America. Meanwhile, her residence in Trinidad, Jamaica, Barbados, Grenada, and Tobago makes for telling insights into the subtle but also glaring differences among these island cultures. Her personal testimony of the socio-economic and structural innovations in revolutionary Grenada and the regime's fateful dissolution is both gripping and harrowing.

Dumas' story carries the reader along by a strong narrative style, with its command of a clear but sophisticated and concise turn of expression. Apart from the public figures whose thought and actions have impacted her life, Dumas also pays homage to her husbands and personal friends who shaped important facets of her self-understanding, especially with regard to the significance of communication and teamwork in the sustenance of personal relationships. But no one is more significant than her mother, the nurse Adeline MacNeill Dumas, whose early feminist resolve so markedly stamped Regina's dogged pursuit of personal happiness. So, the title, *Memoir of a Cocoa Farmer's Daughter*, is remarkable since it is a paean, instead, to Regina's father whom she hardly knew personally, but whose vision of economic independence she consciously mirrors in her reformation of his cocoa estate in Tobago into her present home, agri-business, and nature retreat. Her life's journey is therefore a tribute to both parents whose heritage she lovingly acknowledges.

— *Professor Emerita Maureen Warner-Lewis*

❧ Acknowledgements

THOUGH FEW IN number, the persons to whom I owe a great debt of gratitude in the production of this memoir are so valuable to me that I hardly know where my acknowledgements should begin. For many years, I had been toying with the idea of writing a memoir, especially when challenges such as no one else seemed to be experiencing in their lives loomed large in mine. But I was never emboldened to actually put the thought into action, that is, until Frank, my first husband, laid it out to me very convincingly one evening during a visit to Boston to spend some time with my daughter and her family. He invited me out to dinner (he has lived in Boston for a number of years) and in the course of the evening made what I can only describe as a persuasive argument. Having written and published material himself, he offered to proofread whatever I wrote once I emailed it to him. But Frank went beyond the promise of proofreading. More than simply taking responsibility for this aspect, he went further, reminding me of titbits of information I had forgotten, thereby enhancing what I had chronicled. He went beyond simply proofreading as his suggestions improved my writing style overall and when the going got tough for him by way of my recording of memories that were not exactly complimentary to him, he took it all in stride.

Additionally, two persons, now both deceased, played wonderfully supportive roles in the writing of this memoir. Lloyd King, whose vast and intimate knowledge not only of the institution of the University of the West Indies but also of the regional political events and responses of the intelligentsia to the said events, came into the picture at an early stage. Further, Lloyd, whose academic, socio-economic and political interests and experiences spanned several decades (he was actually my lecturer in Spanish at UWI from 1965–68), was able to advance comments which contributed to both content value and the courage I required to continue writing chapter after chapter. He made suggestions for additions which he thought might be useful or omission of some elements which in his view were superfluous. As a result, his input helped with the tightening of the narrative in no uncertain way.

The contribution of the other friend who is also deceased – Roderick Sanatan – was completely unexpected and unsolicited. Roderick, who had sat as a member of my management committee at the Caribbean Network for Integrated Rural Development (CNIRD), had for years been listening to me plan my dream of establishing a retreat deep within the forests of Tobago, the tiny sister isle of Trinidad. When, finally, he arrived to spend some time here at the Retreat and we got to talking about the memoir project, Roderick, who had always worked with governments in the region but whose heart belonged to community-based and non-governmental organizations, agreed that I should send him a copy to read. Roderick did not simply make useful comments on presentation of the material, but went further, rattling off a string of possibilities for distributing and disseminating what he viewed as an important rural and community development tool. Having read the draft, his positive words, coming as they did from someone whom I knew to be a stickler for getting things right, gave me a great deal of encouragement and confidence.

Both Lloyd and Roderick died suddenly and although their deaths were some five years apart, both left me with a sense of utter and complete loss and wondering why? They did not know each other but from my privileged perch they reminded me of each other; both so brilliant, each in his own way, so private, each in his own way, so ready to help and support my project – just because I asked!

As picky as I was about those to whom I sent copies for comment, I knew I wanted the input of Khafra Kambon whose dedication to the cause of political advancement of the Caribbean region in general and the country of Trinidad and Tobago in particular has been unquestionable since the decade of the sixties. Indeed, my specific request to him was to help me beef up the section related to events in 1970. I thought it would be of key importance to the reader of the memoir to have a feel of what was developing with respect to the social consciousness of the society during the latter part of the 1960s and culminating in the events of 1970. For the sake of what Kambon referred to as historical accuracy, the request to him was that he assist with strengthening the perspective, the facts and their sequencing with regard to that period. This he focused on despite his busy schedule.

- *Acknowledgements*

Apart from the fun I had with my niece Danielle Toppin when it came to choosing image combinations for the book covers, I was also deeply impressed by her artistic judgement and expertise – skillfully displayed in the eyecatching imagery and design of the book covers.

Frank was to enter the picture yet again when I considered whom I should ask to write the Foreword. Frank, much to my surprise, suggested someone with whom he had related many years earlier and whom he considered would be of value, mainly because he was aware that she was from my hometown, Tunapuna and, given her academic record, would be a great asset. What Frank was not aware of was that apart from knowing me, Professor Maureen Warner-Lewis had shared a close personal relationship with my mother, despite the age difference between the two women – Mama having helped to nurse her back to health after a serious illness when she was a young girl. Maureen immediately agreed to take on the task of not simply writing the Foreword but, further, that of proofreading the manuscript and giving suggestions for improvement to the style and content of some of the chapters. And if, unlike many new writers, I am the beneficiary of a publisher for whom I have the greatest respect, it is Maureen Warner-Lewis that I must thank.

This publication, as I suppose is the case with most memoirs, has something to do with the accomplishment of dreams emerging out of creative ideas, yes. But, in addition, it has everything to do with growth, with the gaining of experience, with learning and with gratitude. My acknowledgement of all whose names appear above is meant to be a tribute of love and thanks in this regard.

🌿 Prologue

The seemingly straightforward title of this work belies the fact that three clear influences intersected and dominated the course of my life. One of these was the legacy of my father, a cocoa farmer, who sadly died while I was a newborn, just six weeks old. Absent though he was from my life, it was my deceased father's bequest – his world view as much as the material inheritance he left behind in the form of an unencumbered cocoa estate – that ultimately held great sway over what I would finally opt to do with my life. My father Reginald, a black man born at the end of the nineteenth century, mere decades following the abolition of slavery, in a rural village on the tiny island of Tobago, had decided by age 21 that he would invest, not merely in property but in the purchase of a cocoa estate, thereby deeming himself a "planter" – the term used with pride on my baptismal certificate to describe his occupation.

The second and more overt of the two parental influences came from my mother, a nurse by profession and a woman whose strength, determination and force of personality enabled her to single-handedly raise her three children and shape their futures without the help of anyone, whether relative or friend, male or female. However, while my mother is seen as having the foremost impact on my life's trajectory, my father's legacy, seemingly tangential to hers, is not only significant to my development and approach to life, but also helps lay the foundation for what has become the culmination of my life's work.

The third influence enters and almost immediately takes centre stage in a conscious way when inadvertently I am exposed to the principles and practices of rural development in the context of the lives of rural dwellers. My sojourn in Jamaica gave me my first insight into the way of life of rural people via my interaction as a teacher with rural based students and the sometimes painful realities of their existence. I was struck by the huge effort they made to achieve something meaningful with their lives – an effort I had by no means sensed among the urban based secondary school students I had previously taught in Trinidad. However, it was only a few years later when I worked in Geneva with the World Council of Churches (WCC) development programme that this third influence truly emerged. Like a seed watered by the dual strands of parental influence, coupled with the Jamaican teaching experience, my aspirations quietly began to germinate and push through my consciousness, ultimately allowing me to mentally and then actually experience the realization of my dream, built as it was on all my earlier experiences and influences.

These influences all blended into the ultimate creation of an "other" Regina, far removed from the 24-year-old who in 1969 left her native Trinidad and Tobago for Jamaica with the simple thought that she was merely accompanying her husband, Frank, in the fulfillment of *his* academic dream. Her expectation was that she would return to her native shores two years later to continue to lead the ordinary, everyday life usually enjoyed by most middle class-*ish* people. However, it was not back to Trinidad that I would go on the completion of Frank's assignment in Jamaica but rather to Geneva, Switzerland, a scenario against which I railed and did my utmost to avoid. Yet, it was here that, ironically, my grounding with the developing world in general and with the Caribbean and Latin America in particular received its most powerful cut and thrust. This, ultimately, prepared me for the on-the-ground development challenges I was to encounter, taught me how to make required changes and begin the undertaking, in no uncertain terms, of the personal and professional development issues I would encounter.

Was it sheer good luck that not only led me to Geneva, but also to the World Council of Churches and the opportunity to work with a mentor in the person of Dr. Julio de Santa Ana, Uruguayan political scientist, Christian Marxist and development activist? I like to think that it was. I like to reflect on the fact that my latent intellectual potential benefitted and was in fact awakened and fired up by persons like Frank, the student I met in my very first trimester at the University of the West Indies and subsequently married – Frank, a committed scholar of the black re-enterprise – and Julio de Santa Ana, committed development theoretician and activist. Great learning would subsequently come from the Caribbean non-governmental organizations (NGOs) with which I would work, from the grass roots individuals, groups and organizations encountered regionally and internationally whose experiences would teach me so much and give me ideas of how these could be shared with others.

Thus, the tapestry of this account of my life is woven with the threads of events at the personal level as much as at the professional. Interaction with regional and international NGOs – in particular those working in the area of rural development – account for the professional input. If it is true, as someone has said, that we are all "journeying in life in search of something", then it can be said that in my case there was no conscious awareness of "seeking" anything. I was, however, mindful of the fact that I was always discovering something new regarding other peoples, other cultures, other experiences, other truths.

Revolutionary Grenada became part of the experience! What a process! What an "experiment"! It was the best of times. It was the worst of times. Here I was, on the Caribbean island of Grenada in October 1983 continuing to slowly put together the pieces of my life after my marriage to Frank, sadly, had fallen apart in 1980. Appointed as Secretary General of the Agency for Rural Transformation by the Prime Minister himself and his People's Revolutionary Government, I was stolidly serving the first revolution in the Anglophone Caribbean following the advent of national independence, and playing a pivotal role in the unfolding of the Grenada process. Among my closest friends in Grenada, I counted Jacqueline Creft, Minister of Education. It was the best of times.

Then it happened. The Grenada Revolution imploded. On October 19, 1983, not only was Prime Minister Maurice Bishop assassinated by rebellious factions within his People's Revolutionary Government, but so too were many of his closest comrades, Jacqueline Creft included. It was, decidedly, the worst of times.

Who could have imagined the multiple twists and turns that my life would take? I now had no choice but to return, a single parent, to a Trinidad where I had once determined my children would *not* be raised, if only to spare them the exposure to an attitude of materialism and disdain for protection of the environment which I found so prevalent in the society in which I had grown up. But ultimately, it would be these very twists and turns that would provide me with the opportunity for pulling all these strands together to weave the tapestry of my life as working mother and feminist, combined with the passion of a rural community development worker and activist.

If today I have managed to fulfil my dream of becoming the owner and manager of a successful rural enterprise, it is in large measure owing to the lessons learned from the various rural based constituencies with which I have interacted, acquaintance with the intrinsic worth of community, knowledge of the benefits of teamwork, and possession of a personal value system that in the end trumps everything. And, of course, my parents....

It is my hope that the reader will find this account of the course of my life both useful and stimulating.

*My very first photograph – taken at age 9
with my older sister, Marina*

1 ✬ The Early Years

THOUGH PEOPLE TALK about remembering events from when they were four, three or even two years old, I am always sceptical of these claims. My skepticism may be tinged with envy given that my earliest recollection of events and experiences nudge closer to the age of five, maybe.... Sometimes I think my poor recollection of events has to do with the fact that the first photograph of myself was taken when I was nine. Both of my siblings have photographs of themselves as babies or tiny children – I have no idea what I looked like before that family photograph was taken. Even my mother, Adeline, born in 1902, had photographs of herself and her sister under the age of five. I am sympathetic, though, to the situation in which she found herself when, just some six weeks after giving birth to me, my father died of a heart attack, leaving her a single parent of three, the oldest of whom was just ten.

Nothing in my early life had prepared me for a career in rural community development. I was born and grew up in the tiny society of Trinidad and Tobago and in a personal world that was itself tiny in comparison to most families. There were no grandparents, no uncles or aunts, no first cousins, no extended family. No father. There was just my mother, Adeline, my brother Reginald, older than me by ten years and my sister Marina, who had been perfectly content to interact with her sibling, younger than her by two and a half years, until she reached the grand old age of 12 and puberty kicked in. Luckily for me, I discovered that I loved my own company especially after an early introduction to the world of books.

It's not that there weren't any relatives. My mother was the beneficiary of uncles, aunts and first cousins – from both her father's and her mother's sides of her family – which made me the beneficiary of great-uncles, great-aunts and second cousins. But I longed to be like my peers whose parents had siblings who in turn had their own offspring. Things were not helpful on my father's side either. He was the only child of his parents and like

Adeline at age 3 with 2-year-old Marie
on their widowed father's knee

me, was a mere baby when his father died, a young man of 29, drowning off the coast of Parlatuvier in his native Tobago. His mother did remarry and had other children who, it seems, were all deceased by the time I was born. As for my mother, she had lost both parents and her only known sibling by the time she was ten. I say "known" because although there were whispers that my grandfather had fathered two other daughters after the death of his wife, my mother had no idea at the time who they were or where they could be found.

So it was that I languished throughout my childhood and adolescent years wondering why fate had played such a cruel trick on me, a feeling I thought had dissipated over time until my children were born and I found myself continuously reminding them how lucky they were to have two grandmothers (both grandfathers were dead), uncles, aunts and first cousins on both sides of their family.

Adeline — An Early Feminist?

To say that my mother, Adeline, had the single greatest influence on my life is to put it mildly. While typical of most traditional West Indian parenting styles, what made my mother's approach more impactful in my family's case was the fact that she was not simply the greatest but also the only consciously felt influence on our lives. And the distinction did not end there. Certainly, older than the mothers of all my peers (she was 43 when I was born), she was, in retrospect, a surprisingly modern woman in the way that she had put career and financial independence before marriage and the bearing of children. From her teenage years hers were ideas of upward mobility, and with the choices open to women with such notions limited to nursing and to teaching, she chose nursing. In her excellent two-volume study (2008), *The Changing Society of Tobago 1838–1938*, Susan Craig-James notes that in those times census data did not even list the occupation of nursing as a career activity for enumeration. Class II is the category in which it would most likely have fit, including as it did teachers, druggists, overseers, supervisors and the like. However, in the 1901–1946 census, the profession of nursing is not even listed.

There was, perhaps, an explanation for this. According to Adeline, there was absolutely no provision for the formal training of nurses in Tobago. In colonial times, the training of nurses took place in Trinidad only and the few who succeeded in their training tended to remain in Trinidad and not return to Tobago. The "nurses" who existed in Tobago did not just comprise a mere handful, but were, in fact, the recipients of only informal training by doctors who utilized their services as practical assistants. Another perhaps more alarming reason was the fact that once married, a nurse was not only debarred from completing her nursing certification but, even if she had completed it, would not have been eligible for salaried employment with the government of the day.

Marriage, it would seem, was a kind of double-edged sword. On the one hand, while women wanted and were expected to marry and have children, on the other hand, they were also expected to give up working outside of the home once they did. Instead, it was presumed that they would transfer their energies to bearing and raising children, taking care of their husbands' needs and wishes and generally being householder in chief. This meant that those

Adeline! circa 1932

who formerly had jobs (including teachers) had to resign their positions and those who did not, well, they were now officially housebound and forever denied the possibility of earning their own income. Exceptions to this included those married women with abilities such as sewing, bookkeeping or animal husbandry which did not require them to earn a livelihood outside of the home. That was the role, function and responsibility of the husband they married.

My mother, Adeline, was dead certain that this would not, under any circumstances, be her fate! So, when at the age of sixteen she received an offer of marriage from a 40-year-old suitor, the response was clearly a negative one. In a context in which there was no parent to spur her on, no adult to pay particular attention to her well-being or her ambitions for her future, Adeline thus created her own plan for the implementation of the career path she designated herself. Following the death of her parents, she had experienced "transfers" from one relative to another on both her father's and mother's sides of the family, in a place where opportunities for women, especially those living in Tobago, were

Reginald! Always a spiffy dresser – according to Adeline

few and far between. Her getaway plan would mean leaving the place she had called home all her life to reside in another where there were neither relatives nor friends on whom she could rely. This, however, did not deter her. She never openly said so, but I have the impression that her clear decision was to move away from Tobago – a place which had brought her little joy – and settle in Trinidad where she could make a fresh start.

Her meeting with my father, Reginald was quite by chance. Working as a sales clerk at Wilson Store – a dry goods store in Scarborough – while she saved up enough to go to Trinidad to fulfill her ambition, Adeline met Reginald one afternoon when, on a visit home to Tobago from the United States where he lived, he passed by the store to greet a cousin of his who was also employed there. Reginald was smitten and would return time and again until his interest in Adeline was finally and openly declared. Already in her mid-twenties and past the normal age by which a young woman would have been married at the time, Adeline held fast to her life plan: a profession in nursing first, marriage and children after. Reginald was relegated to the waiting area. And wait he did – for five long years until that precious dream was realized.

In retrospect, it would appear that both Adeline and Reginald, from quite different but equally challenging childhood backgrounds, had determined their individual life plans, quite separate from each other, but both prepared to pursue these plans to fruition. Reginald lost his father who had died by drowning while he was a baby, and while his mother had remarried and had other children, Reginald had been close to none of them.

He had journeyed to the United States for the express purpose of working hard and saving his money, which he sent home to an uncle for the purchase of a cocoa estate in Moriah, Tobago. This was an estate to which he later returned to reside, to take on the cultivation of a crop about which he knew little and with experience of which he had none, and all his projections were centred on that goal.

Adeline's story was somewhat different. When she had put together enough money to take her to Trinidad to begin the pursuit of her chosen profession, she secured a recommendation from a cousin who was then the matron in charge of the Scarborough Hospital. She travelled to Trinidad and presented herself before the matron at the then Colonial (now General) Hospital in Port of Spain, wearing her most becoming outfit, and inwardly and outwardly armed with the determination to succeed in her quest. Such determination no doubt must have communicated itself to the matron. The interview was successful, and Adeline was on her way to becoming a nurse.

So, Reginald waited and Adeline studied. Reginald transferred the deed to the estate to his name, and Adeline won a silver medal for placing second in her final nursing examinations. In 1932, the marriage too was secured when Adeline was 30 and Reginald 39. The patient Reginald was, however, made to wait a further two years before his wife could join him in the United States where he still resided. Adeline had decided that to complete her nursing qualifications she needed to have, in addition to general nursing, certification in midwifery.

It was an approach that she would continue to apply – this sense of ambition in career choice, and the exercise of personal development and discipline in raising her children – in an undertaking in which she was the sole comptroller, the sole arbiter. When my father died, no other male presence, indeed no other person of influence in our lives was ever to appear on the scene.

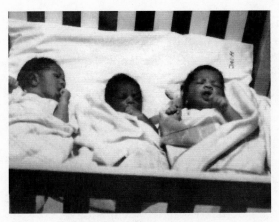

Adeline home-delivers triplets –
single-handedly, circa 1944

Her mental strength and single-mindedness of purpose would once more be made manifest in the recounting of events surrounding my birth. As the sole district midwife in Chaguanas in Central Trinidad, there was no question of her having a home delivery and therefore it was to the Port of Spain hospital that she would be admitted. But she had delayed her departure by several hours because of a reluctance to leave my dying father's bedside. Finally, she contacted the taxi driver, Mr. Barakat Ali, who by prior arrangement would take her to the hospital. Well, I was almost born en route. "Faster, Barakat Ali, faster!" – she urged this poor man, who no doubt had visions of an event which no driver anywhere could possibly wish to happen in the vehicle he used to ply his trade. Moreover, there was no one accompanying her so what would be his role? When, finally, the nervous driver deposited her at the entrance to the hospital, she sped down the corridor (as best she could no doubt) shouting, "Baby, nurse, baby!" Two days later she discharged herself despite the pleadings of the doctor, but she did so with no remorse. She did not simply have a young baby but a very sick husband and a toddler at home who needed her to be there.

Reginald too had a life story worthy of note. Unlike Adeline, he lost only one of his parents but, as he told her, his childhood was unhappy because his mother appeared to favour his step-siblings, pretty much leaving him to fend for himself. When, as a young man he left Tobago to seek his fortune in the United States of America, he had a distinct goal in mind since he saved and sent money to an uncle to pay for the purchase of a small cocoa estate which would eventually become his own. In the work by Susan Craig-James, *The Changing Society of Tobago, 1838–1938*, referenced above, she underscores the fact that between 1900 and1940 the most important social change which had taken place in Tobago was that it had become "a society of landowners, raising the general level of security and well-being and softening the dividing lines between planter and labourer". It must therefore have been with an infinite sense of pride that Reginald wrote the word "planter" on his younger children's baptismal certificates in the column designated for the naming of the parents' respective occupations.

My own baptismal certificate with my father's occupation described
(3rd col. from right) as "Planter" – a term he used with pride

In listening to the narratives related by my mother, two things about my father struck me. First, that he was obviously a risk-taker. He didn't simply take the risk of going off to a strange land where he knew no one and had no job lined up, but he also clearly had a plan that the American interlude would be just that, a means by which he could return to his homeland to pursue an occupation of which he knew nothing – cocoa farming – not as an employee but an employer, an entrepreneur. Indeed, the entrepreneurial spirit seemed to have been imbued in him since years later he actually purchased houses in the Chaguanas district (in Trinidad) where Adeline lived and rented them to various tenants. He told her that, never mind Chaguanas was in the late thirties and early forties a sleepy little rural village, he could tell that one day it would become a thriving district and he wanted to get on board at an early stage. He died in 1945, several years before Chaguanas would, in fact, entirely fulfill the prophecy he had made on its behalf.

The second thing that strikes me about him is the fact that this man, born in the 1800s, actually agreed to wait until the woman he sought to marry was ready to marry him. Further, that he agreed to commute between Tobago and Trinidad when, the marriage having taken place, Adeline refused to live on his estate in Tobago, preferring instead to practise her nursing career in Trinidad. He too, seemed to have been surprisingly modern in his outlook for a man of his times!

Returning, however, to my theory of Adeline's feminism, while we lived in Chaguanas where she was the district nurse and midwife, my brother was a pupil of the Chaguanas Government School. Native of Tobago though she was, she had researched the school system to determine which was the best for her son and decided that my brother would go to none other than Queen's Royal College in Port of Spain. His initial effort at the Exhibition Examination, as it was then called, did not earn him a scholarship. He did, however, win a place at the Naparima College in San Fernando but this did not satisfy Adeline's ambitions. She made him repeat the year and take the exam again, this time with the result she wanted. Too far in those times to travel daily between Chaguanas and Port of Spain, Reggie was boarded in Port of Spain during the week, returning home on weekends. He would later reward Adeline's efforts by winning an Island Scholarship in 1953.

We moved to Tunapuna when I was about four years old and, equally determined that the same opportunities be extended to her daughters as to her son, she enrolled us both at the Tunapuna E.C. School which at the time had a stellar reputation for success at the Exhibition Examination. When it was my sister's turn to take this examination, in Adeline's view, Marina's grades were not up to standard and thus she sought a meeting with the headmaster to discuss what could be done. To her utter dismay and anger, he indicated to my mother that not all her children "could be Island scholars" and suggested that she accept the grades Marina was getting. Furious, my mother did not simply remove Marina from the school, she moved me out as well – no discussion, no fanfare. The next thing I knew, I was attending Duke St. Girls E.C. School in Port of Spain one year before I was due to take the Exhibition Examination. Marina was sent to Tranquillity Girls Intermediate School.

I was bewildered by Port of Spain. What did a young girl from a semi-rural area (as Tunapuna was considered to be in those times) know about it except for the once yearly Christmas shopping outings or the occasional visits to family and friends in Belmont? Tunapuna is some 8 miles from Port of Spain and the train was my mother's transport of choice. Perhaps though the decision was pre-determined by the family of the girl, Aileen Dolly, who was selected to be my companion of sorts. She was already attending the Port of Spain school and could accompany me on the train rides and walks to the school. Apart from that, I was on my own.

The following year I sat the Exhibition Examination and won no scholarship. But Adeline had hedged her bets. She had also enrolled me to take the Entrance Examination to Bishop Anstey High School, her secondary school of choice for me. The gamble paid off and I was admitted to Bishops, one year younger than everyone else in my class and not by any means prepared either for high school or for meeting another set of new people in another new environment – for the second year in a row. Once again, it was Adeline's choice that was to prevail and for better or for worse, my tenure at Bishop Anstey High School began.

It must have been in my second year at Bishops that I discovered, to my utter dismay, that my mother was absolutely serious about me becoming a doctor. You know, I did understand that she had ambitions for her children and I knew that Reggie had disappointed her by deciding that medicine was not going to be his career of choice. But to think, even remotely, that Regina would somehow be expected to step up to the plate and fulfill that particular dream of hers was, to say the least, wishful thinking in the extreme. To begin with, I was an unremarkable student at best although I had always done well at English and discovered in high school that I loved foreign languages as well. But math and science were no friends of mine and when, in the third form I was not even allowed to include biology among my subjects (they had noticed that I certainly could not handle even general science) my relief was palpable and my excuse official. Adeline's disappointment was bitter – there would be no doctor in the family. She had certainly never bothered to ask me what I wanted to do with my life. Not that I would have known since I had never considered it. All I dreamed about was leaving school, getting a job, earning money to secure my independence from a mother who knew how to keep a firm grip on her minor children.

The Growing Up Years

Boyfriends, of whom she knew nothing, saved the day for me. Studies were secondary to the issue of having some fun in life. And there was a fair succession of them – William, Earl, Michael (in that order), all polite and well-meaning guys who showed me a respect (of which Adeline would have approved, if not of the relationships themselves) and friendship which helped me through my teenage years in the absence of any male presence in my otherwise female dominated life. My brother, shortly after the return from his four-year stint at Cambridge, had married and moved on. As for my mother, she did not have a single male friend and, as earlier indicated, there was no father or uncle or male cousins from whom perspectives could be obtained, analyses made or conclusions drawn. The boyfriends were therefore used to fill the gap.

I was fifteen years old when we finally moved into our own home. No more rentals, no more landlords coming to inspect the premises and collect rents, no rules as to what could or could not be done on the premises, no repairs to remain untended while the property owner dealt with his or her own priorities. This was ours. The houses that my father had left us in Chaguanas had finally been sold and Adeline was using the proceeds of those sales towards the purchase of the new acquisition. Park Lane, as we grew to call it, though a modest, three-bedroom cottage, was grand and beautiful in our eyes, if only because of what it signified. Like most of the events in Adeline's life, however, this had been no easy victory. She had purchased the house while it was relatively new but occupied by a tenant – a young man who was always smiling but who made my mother cry a great deal. Hers were tears of anger and frustration at the many stumbling blocks he placed in her path, simply to avoid moving out of the house that she had made so much effort to purchase. She took the matter to the court and won her case after the third appearance.

In the end, I shocked my teachers and myself by doing well enough at the Senior Cambridge examination to continue on to sixth form, thus delaying my plan to get a job to earn me some money. I still had no idea – nor did I spend time dwelling on it – what I would ultimately do with my life at either the personal or professional level. It would be my love of reading that would finally propel me in the direction of the Central Library where I worked for one year, thoroughly enjoying my access to the rare works of Caribbean fiction housed in the reference section of the library. It was then that my mother dropped another bombshell: it was time to take my studies further and apply for entry into the University of the West Indies (UWI). Huh? Just when I had begun to enjoy my newfound freedom of earning and spending a monthly salary of TT$120 (US$20) which allowed me to travel via first class on the train (a monthly ticket cost TT$5), give her an allowance, save a monthly sum and spend the rest on myself? Why would I give up all of this to attend UWI? What would I study there anyway? I still had no plans for my life!

Adeline, however, was not to be deterred. Dr. Eric Williams, then Prime Minister of Trinidad and Tobago, had done my mother a huge favour by making both secondary and tertiary education free and that opportunity would not be allowed to slip through her fingers! Sulkily I complied, and then sought a way to repay her for what I perceived as her continued domination of my life. After all I was almost 20!

The perfect solution presented itself. I would not choose any particular career path, I would simply continue to study the subjects I had done in sixth form – French, Spanish and English – and let the chips fall where they may. Thus, triumphant, I entered the University of the West Indies in September of 1965 armed with a determination, not so much to succeed academically as much as to have a good time while pursuing subjects with which, I thought, I was already familiar. I was preparing to enjoy my youth and my life, entering a phase of which I was totally ignorant and for which I could not care less.

In retrospect, I wonder why is it that I had no ambitions for myself, especially being part of a household where the "head honcho" took it all so seriously and communicated this approach to her children. But it wasn't just about career that I was clueless. I was part of a society of which I knew nothing, and I reflected on nothing. For example, I took no interest in the lives of my mother's domestic helpers, never wondered about notions of disparity in the society, never read anything in the newspaper except the comic strip, and when Dr. Eric Williams began his famous "University of Woodford Square" lectures, there was no interest on my part in what he had to say. Although I didn't realize it at the time, I was living in my own little bubble....

The high school curriculum did not help either. The history I studied was British and European, the geography was geared to temperate countries, the literature was Shakespeare, Dickens and Austen, and the families in our Spanish text books were from Spain and not Latin America. Even the cookery was British, taught as we were by an Englishwoman who focused on roast beef and Yorkshire pudding, white sauces and scones (all of which, by the way, I tried out on my family at home). To be fair, this was the late fifties into early sixties and nationalism, pushed as it was by Premier and, later, Prime Minister Dr. Eric Williams, had not yet taken root in the consciousness, far less the institutions of the country. Our examinations and therefore curricula were set by Cambridge and London Universities, and so an educational institution which wanted the best for its students strove to comply, not simply by teaching the curriculum as best they could, but also by employing foreign graduate teachers who, perhaps, at the time were more available than local college graduate teachers.

This might well have been the thinking of Dr. Williams in his pursuit of improved and higher levels of education when, along with the introduction of free tertiary education to the citizens of the country, he also established the College of Arts and Sciences on the St. Augustine campus. Here was an excellent means of improving the local teaching stock of the country. The education was free once a national qualified for entry and one was guaranteed a job within the teaching system on graduation, especially as the introduction and establishment of government secondary schools offering free secondary education opened up literally several hundred teaching jobs within the country by the mid-1960s.

Although I hardly could have imagined it at the time, I too would enter the teaching service on my graduation in 1968.

2 ❧ Studies, Love and Marriage

Historical Antecedents of UWI

By 1961, AS A RESULT of decisions taken by the governments of the region to expand the academic offerings of the University College of the West Indies (UCWI), each campus (located in Mona, Jamaica; Cave Hill, Barbados; and St. Augustine, Trinidad, respectively) boasted a specialty degree offering or offerings peculiar to itself. This meant that any prospective student from the region, wishing to obtain a degree in that specialty would need to attend the particular campus where it was being offered. Thus, the specialty at Mona was medicine, at Cave Hill it was law, and at St. Augustine the Imperial College of Tropical Agriculture (ICTA) "formed the core of the first Faculty at the new UCWI campus, the Faculty of Agriculture (1960), followed in 1961 by the Faculty of Engineering" (Bridget Brereton, *UWI TODAY*, 10 October, 2010). In 1963 the Government of Trinidad and Tobago went further by introducing a College of Arts and Sciences where teaching in the arts, social sciences and natural sciences began.

Small by international standards, the now revealed beauty of the St. Augustine campus was a source of wonder and surprise to me who, having grown up virtually in its shadow, was nevertheless completely unfamiliar with what was behind those walls, so to speak. The ICTA had been in existence and located at the St. Augustine campus since 1922, but this was not a place to which persons who had no business there ventured – the surrounding communities, over time, had become used to seeing within their environs lots of bespectacled and sandaled Caucasians who were known to be researching the mysteries of cocoa, sugarcane and other crops native to our environment.

The wonder and surprise at the campus' physical beauty was now further reinforced and extended, one might say, by a sense of "West Indian-ness" which was being developed in a way that the attempt at a West Indies Federation had failed to do in the fifties into the early sixties. This new sense of self, so to speak, made campus life interesting, creating opportunities for cultural exchanges, for friendships which in some cases led to marriage and a further transfer of cultural opportunities. To date, the various campuses of the University of the West Indies continue to attract students from all over the region and play a role in training the professional cadres so needed in Caribbean development.

My Studies Commence

In September 1965, I commenced my freshman year at the St. Augustine campus, bent on pursuing a major in French and Spanish but equally determined to have a good time. It was the peripheral (but compulsory) subjects known as survey courses which intrigued and interested me the most: Use of English, Comparative Religion, West Indian History. Despite the firm plans I had made, I found myself actually looking forward to the classes in these courses. I was intrigued for different reasons. Why the "use" of English? Wasn't it something that you just used, once the situation required it? Our lecturer herself was also a source of great interest to me, and so well schooled in the subject she taught that quietly she made a fan of me without ever knowing it. A white Canadian with an East Indian surname, Mrs. Mahabir was the stuff that legends are made of. Articulate, knowledgeable and pregnant, her hair always caught up in a bun, she stunned me and most of the student body by going on Easter vacation leave in 1966, large with the child she was bearing, only to return at the beginning of the new term, two or three weeks later, no longer pregnant and continuing to teach her classes as if no major or immensely significant event had taken place in the intervening period.

In years to come, although at the time I neither could nor would have guessed it, when I became a teacher of the English and Spanish languages, it was mainly what I had learned in the Use of English classes that would stand me in good stead. I found that it really is impossible to teach a foreign language or for that matter the English language unless you have a good grasp and understanding of standard English – the use of English. *Straight and Crooked Thinking* (1953) by Robert H. Thouless was the main text which taught the principles of argumentation and logic.

A second survey course which fascinated me and opened up my mind in a way that has never deserted me since was Comparative

Religion. I would not have imagined that Islam and Christianity had so much in common, for example. Certainly, I would not have guessed that Hinduism is such a practical religion that it can have a global impact on all, regardless of their faith or lack thereof. For a while, my Christian beliefs were wholly abandoned while I delved into the logic and intricacies of religions to which, until then, I had been a total stranger. And I must confess that once I emerged, I was no longer nor could I ever be the same person. The concept of *Atman* – the individual self or eternal soul – essential to the understanding of the foundational principles of Hinduism, of reincarnation, of karma, now widely spoken of, understood and accepted principles and beliefs introduced to me in my first academic year, would unwittingly change the course of my thinking forever.

Not that I realized it at the time. Though these concepts appeared to me to make sense at one level and appealed to my active imagination at another level, I made no conscious attempt to apply them to my thinking or lifestyle. Yet, today, over fifty years later, I can attest to the fact that they never went away and that little by little, my thinking and my lifestyle have been modifying subconsciously to reflect the application of these principles.

We studied Caribbean history, albeit at a superficial level since it was not a main study course. It awakened in me the recognition that I had gained a distinction at high school in a subject which was for the most part alienating in the way it had been taught. History, as seen through the eyes of the British and the Europeans, really did not take into account the culture and mores of the indigenous peoples whom they found here, nor their obvious courage and demonstrated strength in attempting to fight against an oppressor who arrived with such formidable weaponry and manpower as only the wildest imagination could have conjured up. Nor did it ever pay homage to the myriad and admirable ways utilized by enslaved people in the various colonies of the Caribbean to react to the situations of domination and dependence in which they found themselves.

Sadly, I was but mildly interested in the subjects which were to be my majors. I was studying West Indian literature for the first time and Vidia Naipaul was on the syllabus. It was clearly with a sense of deep puzzlement that the lecturer, an Englishman (whose name and the consistent colour of the clothes he wore reflected his ethnic origins) spent the better part of a term trying to get his students to understand what a genius Naipaul really is, how brilliant his work and how objective rather than subjective we needed to be in order to appreciate the writings of this son of the soil. In the end he succeeded with me, at any rate, and I was finally able to read Naipaul without feeling the hairs of my neck bristle.

Naipaul, as I have finally come to understand him, is a creature of the world (his own world?) with no real sense of belonging to any particular geographic or cultural origins. *The Enigma of Arrival*, as close as one gets to an autobiographical treatise, was the work which really opened my eyes to the man and the writer, and in retrospect, it is the truthfulness with which he clearly feels compelled to write, whether about himself or about others, that makes him stand apart from other Caribbean writers. It is also this truthfulness which many find difficult to accept in his various works.

Quietly sitting in the reading room of the University library one afternoon, some two months after I had begun my degree course, no doubt engrossed in the mysteries of comparative religion, I was approached by a young man who politely asked if he could "borrow a pen" since his had suddenly run dry. With the good manners taught me by Adeline, I complied and returned to my reading. I had never seen this student before. Returning the borrowed item about an hour or so later, a conversation was struck up, which again was the polite thing to do. And that, I thought, was the end of that. Little did I know that it merely signalled the end of a beginning.

Frank Taylor, as his name turned out to be, had certain set ideas, which it never occurred to me that someone at the age of 21 would have. He knew, for example, that he was going to excel at his first degree studies and go on to do both master's and PhD degrees. Having attained these, he was going to become a university lecturer in history and help to expose what he referred to as the "intellectual idiocracies" which masked this neo-plantation order he saw as our current socio-economic organization. The term was coined by him to describe the hypocrisy and dishonesty of most of those who up to then had written the history of the islands.

I suppose my disbelief at all these plans was based, not only on my own limited view of the world and the role I had carved out for myself therein, but also the fact that I had not, up till then, encountered at close range anyone who was so intensely interested in things academic. Perhaps the closest I had come was to my brother who had studied abroad but who had returned home for only a very short time before he married and went off once more to far-off places, this time to pursue a diplomatic career. All of this had happened at a time when I was struggling with puberty and adolescence and clearly not mindful of anything approaching future undertakings of any sort.

Thus, to hear a 21-year-old boldly and confidently carve out a life plan which sounded more remote than a dream, certainly filled me with curiosity if not intrigue. But there was more. These were not plans that someone had put into his head – these were his own, born out of a context in which his mother, similarly losing a husband to heart disease and with four young children to care for, had merely tried to educate all her children with the help of her mother and her sister, without pushing them in any particular direction. When at an early age the young Frank showed his natural inclination to excel academically by winning a government exhibition and gaining entry to St. Mary's College, the whole family went out to bat for him. It became a favourite story of his to tell that if there was one egg left in the house, it was understood that he would have it – he needed it to study. And study he did.

Until I met Frank I would not have known that students in Trinidad and Tobago studied Greek! He studied Greek, Latin and French at sixth form, and while he passed with flying colours, he planned to have his studies at university take a completely different turn. History and economics, subjects he had never before studied, would be those in which he would major. Hmmm....

I won't pretend that I was not impressed, not to the point of spurring me on to greater academic heights myself, mind you, but I was impressed all the same. Frank was also not at all hesitant about questioning what most accepted as the basic principles of faith on which Christianity was founded and sustained. Frankly, I thought his attack on the teachings of the church sacrilegious and said so. When he countered by putting to me, as he had apparently done to his religious teachers and leaders, questions which could not be responded to on the basis of logic and proof, I had no choice but to allow him the benefit of his private conclusions.

There was also his politics. Emerging out of an urban social background which highlighted, even more than mine had, the extremes between those who had and those who hadn't, those who had social and money power and those who hadn't, Frank never tired of telling stories which illustrated and underscored these differences as they had impacted on his life and that of his family. His fertile mind and quick intellect naturally led to the support of a political system which would profess and manifest a greater sense and reality of equality among all the peoples of Trinidad and Tobago. Fidel Castro was the exemplar par excellence of this modality and it was therefore no real surprise that in years to come his PhD thesis would be written on the political dynamics of the Cuban revolutionary experience. It was no surprise either that he, along with others of similar bent, would make a successful bid for the opportunity to run the Students' Guild with a view to having it operate along lines of greater equality and opportunity for all.

But there was more to my life on campus than Frank Taylor. Well, I tried to make it that way, to remain true to the promise I had made to myself to study minimally and have a good social time. I made quite a few new friends, particularly among those fortunate enough to be living in student residence on campus. These happy souls did not have to get home at a time considered reasonable, nor give any explanation to anyone as to why they might be late. They could attend Uwee (as we affectionately referred to UWI) meetings and parties – especially the latter – with no parent or guardian being any the wiser regarding the time they got back to their respective rooms. They ate lunch in the dining hall, for example, and then repaired to their rooms to rest while the nonresidents either went home to lunch, usually walking in sun or rain, or bought and ate food on campus only to return to the dismal library or lecture room afterwards, unless one wanted to hang around a noisy student common room where everyone had a view to be loudly expressed.

I believe I tried to take my newly recognized self-confidence one step further and in keeping with the promise I had made to myself, and while I was in my first year accepted the invitation of a male third-year student to attend a carnival fete which was being held on campus. Naturally my girlfriends knew and there was no one else on campus I was obligated to tell. That's what I thought. Wasn't I young, single and unattached? Two days after my "date", on the Monday afternoon, Frank requested a conference – he had something very serious to discuss.

Displaying absolutely no bad attitude or anger, thus taking the wind completely out of my sails given that I was sparring for a fight, Frank politely faced me. Nervously twisting his hands and expressing hurt and disappointment that I had made such a move, he intimated that in his view he had thought that there was something special between us. What was a girl to say? Moved by guilt and now regret at having hurt his feelings, I found myself promising that it would not happen again – although I really did have a good time at the party.

Impact of Global Events on the Caribbean: the Black Power Movement

The 1960s represent a period when, globally, students were taking an interest in things political and expressing their feelings in no uncertain terms. Many events and changes were taking place all around the world and students reacted by creating movements which were anti-war, anti-imperialist, anti-capitalist, anti-racist and on the whole, very militant. Decolonization became the order of the day, not merely in the Caribbean but also in Africa, with the latter having strong resonance within the Caribbean. The Civil Rights Movement in the United States assumed centre stage and Malcolm X became a hero to many. Students in the United States were protesting the Vietnam War and when in November of 1965 Ian Smith proclaimed his Unilateral Declaration of Independence in Northern Rhodesia, now Zimbabwe, there were protests in front of the British High Commission in which UWI students participated, wearing their gowns to ensure their contribution as a new and significant group in the society was recognized.

By 1966 the Black Power Movement in the United States had had a powerful impact on the Caribbean region. On the campus, the rallying cry "Black is Beautiful" was one which had a particular impact on young black people who up to then had borne an awareness that their blackness was something which, while they accepted it, had nonetheless not worked particularly in their favour. Thus, the recognition that blackness was something of beauty and to be proud of played a major role in the self-assertiveness and self-esteem which began to emerge at the time among the majority of Trinidad's youthful population, myself among them.

Finally, I was beginning to truly take notice of myself as an individual and of the world around me. Included among the swirl of grievances which emerged at that time, there also began a move to analyse and report on the ethnic types and/or attendant skin colours which were being selected for which jobs outside of the public sector. Indeed, a study done by Acton Camejo, a University of the West Indies lecturer in sociology confirmed that skin colour was a factor in hiring practices in major private sector institutions. Another study done by Camejo on the local business elite indicated that only 4% of this group was Afro-Trinidadian and 9% Indo-Trinidadian. The rest were predominantly white and "off white" ("nearly white") with a strong representation of Chinese (cf. Camejo's *Racial Discrimination in Employment in the Private Sector in Trinidad and Tobago: A Study of the Business Elite and the Social Structure* published in 1970 by the Institute of Social and Economic Studies, UWI).

A critical target of the Black Power Movement was the foreign dominance of the economy with local whites seen and portrayed as junior partners in this power structure. Thus, generally, the fight against foreign domination, economically, culturally and politically, was at the core of the Black Power struggle. Revolutionary thinking and defiant rhetoric, ideas, ideology and actions thus began to gestate within the region, fueled by the powerful writings of the likes of Frantz Fanon and Paulo Freire. Meanwhile, the Cuban Revolution had begun to make an impact and iconic individuals like Che Guevara had begun to stir the political inventiveness of the youthful intelligentsia. Students who expected to be taken seriously on political questions would not be caught without a copy of Mao Tse-Tung's *Little Red Book* among their private reading list, for the Chinese Revolution too was also having a growing impact on social and political thought in the Caribbean.

It was because of all these events that regionally and locally there emerged a plethora of groups which ran the gamut from academic to radical trade union to Black Power activists to grassroots – all with an activist inclination. Not surprisingly, given what was happening globally, the UWI Guild of Undergraduates also began a process of radicalization from as early as 1966 and by 1968 under the leadership of the late Makandal Daaga, began to reach out toward the wider society, organizing "academic classes" in many parts of Laventille, John John and elsewhere. Struggles for student representation on the various governing bodies of the university, which achieved a high level of success, further radicalized the student body throughout the region. Another student who was to emerge as a leading figure on the campus and in the social upheaval which followed was Khafra Kambon, who was later co-opted to the Guild Council in the post of Publications Chairman.

Interestingly, much of the early political thinking and activity of that era, culminating in the Sir George Williams affair in Montreal, Canada and which was intensely aired and immensely supported on the St. Augustine campus, stimulated the emergence of the National Joint Action Committee (NJAC). NJAC went public with their support of the cause of the students at Sir George Willliams University as well as their resistance to local attempts at purging the University of the West Indies of its radical elements. This followed the incident in which the Canadian Governor General, Sir Roland Michener, and his entourage which included the Governor General of Trinidad and Tobago, Sir Solomon Hochoy, were blocked by students from entering the campus in February of 1969. Such unprecedented action created great national uproar along with ideological debate. This resulted in mass turnouts for the public meetings organized by NJAC which followed. When, in 1969 the National Joint Action Committee established itself as an organization, Frank naturally became an early member but soon left the country to pursue graduate studies at the UWI Mona campus in Jamaica.

Nineteen seventy marked the launch of NJAC onto the national arena and its unambiguous leap into the psyche of every sector of the national community. In February of 1970, in response to the events at the Sir George Williams in which several West Indian students were arrested, the NJAC leadership organized and led a series of marches through Port of Spain as a show of support for the embattled students. The arrest of some of the NJAC protesters for what was described as "disorderly conduct" and "anti-state activism" only served to make their cause public, and gave the leadership the opportunity to raise the broader socio-economic concerns which had become their rallying cry.

Meanwhile Maturity Takes a Forward Step!

All these happenings and expressions of views prompted many verbal exchanges between Frank and me over the period of the years on campus, with me usually at the losing end. By 1964, Frank's mother and siblings had migrated to the United States leaving just him and his aunt occupying the family house, his beloved grandmother having died some years earlier. On the home front, verbal exchanges progressed to introductions and home visits. Adeline surprised us all (herself included no doubt) by developing a distinct affection for Frank. He became a beneficiary of her special Tobago food which he had never before experienced, born and bred as he was in St. James, principally of Trinidadian lineage. When Frank eventually summoned the courage to discuss with Adeline the notion of marriage to Regina, her affection for him did not prevent her from sternly informing him that she had sent her daughter to university to obtain not a husband but a degree. Frank, like Reginald, would have to wait.

I had never been a close friend of anyone from the Port of Spain area, all my friends having come from the rural and suburban districts of the east/west corridor. This so-called "corridor" is the main artery which links the easterly to the westerly districts on the island of Trinidad. In the sixties those east of Port of Spain were considered rural or semi-rural. Now, interestingly, I was the beneficiary of information which allowed me to compare my life with that of someone from "town". It amazed me, for example, that someone from Port of Spain would have seldom ventured as far east as St. Augustine or would almost never have taken a train ride. Taking a girl out on a date meant taking her away from the rural area into the bright lights of the capital, never mind that the cinemas in the rural districts might be showing the same movies as those in Port of Spain. The rotis (a popular East Indian dish but embraced by all races in Trinidad and Tobago) obtained anywhere might taste the same, but that special person in your life had to be treated to a St. James roti.

Frank functioned quite differently from me in respect of his campus friendships. He was one of an inseparable group of five, all of whom had attended St. Mary's College and whose social and ethnic backgrounds were almost a mirror image of the society as it was then and continues to be now. One of them owned a car and they all, with the exception of Lloyd, who studied languages, not only studied the same subjects, but also travelled together without fail between Port of Spain and St. Augustine. So much so that when Frank's amorous responsibilities required walking me home and he was not in place at the appointed time, they would pull up in front of my mother's house to fetch him. They ate lunch together as well, at a Chinese restaurant in Tunapuna. One day, perhaps with a view to checking me out at close range, they invited me to have lunch with them.

The "special" was naturally ordered with extra rice. When the meal was served, I noticed that no one made a move but instead they all invited me to help myself. But while I helped myself to one dish or another, no one else followed suit. "These guys are really polite", I thought to myself. Having helped myself to what I wanted, one of them said, "Finished, Regina?" "Yes," I replied. "You're sure?" they all chorused as a man. Then I saw what the polite waiting had all been about. Those guys, every last one of them, fell on that food with such energy that in less than a minute every single platter was clean, the contents now having been transferred to their individual plates. It was only after my shock had worn off that I could appreciate the experience and laugh about it.

They remained friends too, long after the degrees had been obtained and each moved on to his own preferred life venture. Indeed, it was through the intervention and assistance of one of the group, Peter, that Frank eventually lived his dream of going to study for his PhD in Switzerland, the place where, for me, it all started. It was there that I came to recognize the attitudes of domination and dependence as practised within and between countries and how rural communities, in particular, continue to be affected by these practices.

Friendship with Frank progressed to marriage in 1968, once the degree had been obtained. A teaching job was given preference over one in librarianship but only because the former paid the handsome sum of TT$450 as against $350 at the library. In 1968, $100 was a great deal of money and could make a big difference in the savings of one who had a goal in mind. Jamaica was on the horizon and while I planned to work while Frank studied on a university scholarship, I was entirely uncertain of what I would be doing given that I still had no career choice in mind! My social and ethical consciousness had begun to mature but there were still no life goals established. Saving was thus a key factor in the whole scenario.

I surprised myself by actually enjoying the teaching assignment at St. James' Secondary School in Port of Spain although the third formers were quite a handful. Third formers, I was to discover as time went on, are a special group within any high school student body. They have been in the school system long enough to feel at home, are at the age where their bodies begin to respond to various stimuli, and sufficiently distanced from their major school leaving examination to believe that time is on their side. In a co-educational institution such as St. James' Secondary was, the challenges rose several notches especially for me, just a few years older than they were and, in most instances, definitely not as tall.

It was for me an occasion of pure surprise and pleasure when, some 25 years later, in the course of my NGO development work in Trinidad, I stumbled across one of these former students, then and up to the time of writing these memoirs, a senior person in one of the government ministries. He recognized me and it was interesting to catch up by way of exchanging perspectives from that year that I taught his class. It would seem that I had done a good job of masking my fear, not so much of them – most of them were taller and stronger than I was – but rather my fear of failing to demonstrate to them that I knew my subject matter (I was their Spanish teacher) and that I was determined that they as well as I should succeed in our respective endeavours.

That first year of marriage brought so much into my life that was new and unexpected that it continues to stand out as a sort of beacon in my memory. Here was I, having satisfied Adeline not just with the basic requirement of a first degree but with a husband and, from my perspective, the opportunity to be mistress of my own life in the bargain. With some reluctance, I had now transferred to urban life and we together earned enough to purchase a used Austin 1100 in fairly good condition. Frank had just obtained his driver's license and I was in the process of securing mine. Our St. Ann's neighbours were all very friendly, welcoming us into the community of the little cul-de-sac in which we lived. Some of the friends we made there were to become friends for life.

Imagine not having to ask permission to go anywhere, to go out and return home as late as one liked, to just decide to go for a drive on a Sunday and end up perhaps at the other end of the island. Night time outings around Queen's Park Savannah for coconut water and oysters were a special treat, as were moonlight drives to Carenage Bay to take a dip in the ocean with David and Cynthia – two of our neighbours turned friends. Stopping by a standpipe at 9 o'clock in the evening to clandestinely wash the salt from Carenage off our bodies sent us into hysterics. I think it was the sheer freedom and pleasure which these actions represented that ensured that we did it on a regular basis. Imagine, too, shopping at new and fancy urban supermarkets *without a list* and with someone to help push the trolley (albeit somewhat reluctantly) piled with merchandise in the bargain! As for Adeline? Well, she surprised me by making not even the tiniest effort to intervene in my new lifestyle.

That was the time in my life when I started to take on responsibilities in a serious way, although not consciously. I had not had the experience of observing or being either the wife or teacher I now was and there were no tips to be offered by anyone. I took on my teaching assignment with relish and flair, determined that the students should not find out that, deep inside, I was really frightened of making mistakes. I regularly gave homework and tests, and piles of exercise books and test papers, marked, to be marked or in the process of being marked could always be found on the dining table of our apartment. Many were the occasions when I took issue with Frank's casual approach to teaching. He would bring home for grading the exercises which had been undertaken by his students only to leave them lying untouched for what seemed like weeks!

As for my new role of wife... Adeline had told me nothing. It must have been that she was too shy and though "shy" does not seem to match the personality of the woman I have so far described, I can recall various occasions when she appeared to be timid in her approach to discussions of matters female. It was the rector of the church where we were to be married who thought to ask me, one day following a counselling session, whether my mother had told me "anything" and even he appeared to be too shy to spell out exactly what he meant. For my part, however, with a complete and natural inability to hide my feelings, I was not at all hesitant about acquainting him about my ignorance of these matters. He responded by lending me a book to read. It appeared then that I would not be having the benefit of a heart to heart with anyone nor a question and answer session! Auntie Belle, the great aunt to whom I was closest had never married or lived with any male partner and my godmother, to whom I was quite close, had never married, never had a partner, nor for that matter, any children. So, there I was, left on my own – again – to make the best of my situation.

I took the book – it was useful in its own way – and thought I would then stimulate some reaction from my mother by leaving it next to our newly acquired telephone where she was bound to see it. Nor would I have any qualms about telling her who had loaned it to me! Alas, it was with a heavy heart that I finally removed the book from its temporary resting place – Fr. Douglin needed to have it back and in the interim not a single question had been asked about it.

Thus, confounded on all fronts, I drew on my fairy-tale notions of romance and marriage which were still very much alive in my head and imagination from stories I had been reading since childhood. I cooked, cleaned and washed with an energy which I expected would draw great admiration not to mention verbal appreciation from my new husband. I scoured recipe books with a view to preparing meals which would be delicious and nutritious yet different from the norm. My pride forestalled any notion of asking for an opinion on the culinary efforts. I truly expected them to emerge as a matter of course. But, here again I was to be disappointed. One day, Frank finally noticing that he could barely recognize what he was eating, mildly informed me that he would be perfectly happy if every day I could give him "straight" [only] meat and rice. The metaphorical knife had been plunged and twisted – although quite unknowingly by the perpetrator of the act – signalling the end of my culinary efforts but not before bitter tears of frustration and defeat had been shed in private.

In retrospect, I think that a major part of the problem was the fact that neither Frank nor I had had the experience of living within a so-called nuclear family, given that both fathers had died when we were small children and our mothers had not remarried nor taken up other relationships. In large measure, therefore, we were making things up as we went along without any knowledge or clue as to what the result might be! Reflecting on this in later years, I would realize that all we had needed to do was to communicate, me sharing my views on what I thought my role would be, him sharing his in like fashion, and both of us coming to a conclusion which, even if not perfectly satisfactory to both, would nonetheless be based on mutual knowledge and not guesswork. Honest and open communication is, in my view, perhaps the most important aspect of family life.

My conversion to the preparation of simple dishes from then onwards, however, was so complete that many years later when I started the business which I now manage and finally had the opportunity to display somewhat creative cooking skills, my children were amazed that they had grown up on such simple fare when all along I had the ability to do things differently. But maturity and down-to-earth-ness were beckoning, and I needed to turn my thoughts and sights toward the second new phase in as many years that my life was about to enter. What awaited me on the other side? How would I adjust to life in a totally new society – a life still without any specific goals per se?

3 Jamaica 1969-1972

Social Consciousness Stirs and Develops

IT WAS IN JAMAICA that I first got a peek into a society which displayed notions and attitudes of domination and dependence that I had not experienced in Trinidad. This might well have been either because of my earlier lack of sophistication and awareness or perhaps from being too much a part of that society to view it in the analytical way I could in Jamaica – unfamiliar as it was to me. Similarly, it was in Jamaica that my experience in the field of teaching was raised several notches higher than in urban Trinidad. This was not merely because of the avid interest in learning displayed by the students there but also the respect I grew to have for the way in which these rural-based girls dealt with the life challenges they consistently encountered. Little did I know that in Switzerland the effects of integrating and mingling with my rural Jamaican students, combined with an introduction to development theory, would subconsciously lay the groundwork for an approach to development, changing my thinking forever.

I arrived in Jamaica in September 1969, the trip representing for me the furthest I had ever travelled out of Trinidad and Tobago. Frank had arrived well before me, having elected to use the Federal Maple, one of the two cargo/passenger boats which traversed the region between Jamaica in the north and Trinidad in the south. These two vessels had been a gift to the region from the Canadian government at the time of the declaration of a Federation in 1958 – a Federation which, sadly, failed partly because the larger territories within the region could not agree on a formula which would leave their individual political sense of self-esteem intact. The notion behind the granting of these two vessels was not merely to encourage inter-island trade but also, by combining a passenger-carrying feature, to provide cheaper transport to the peoples of the islands, thus facilitating and encouraging cultural and other exchanges. For Frank, travelling to Jamaica via the Federal Maple was a way to acquaint himself with the islands within the chain, thus expanding his knowledge and horizons as a student of history.

A residence had been secured at Orchid Path in Mona Heights prior to my arrival. Mona Heights, a middle-class enclave built in 1958–59, was situated on the virtual doorstep of the university campus. In the mid to late sixties came the opportunity for the owners of these properties to cash in on the influx of students, both Jamaican and overseas, who were more and more beginning to participate in the expanded university system. What at the time of construction of these dwellings had been considered maids' quarters, were miraculously converted to furnished student accommodations, thereby earning income for the owners instead of their having to provide accommodation for live-in help. For students, it provided the basic accommodation required and easy access to the campus. From Mona Heights one approached the campus via a beautiful old stone aqueduct built in the eighteenth century by the slaves on the Mona Sugar Estate. Two hundred years later this monument is still perfect.

Nothing had prepared me for Jamaica. Its sheer size – two and a half times the size of Trinidad – staggered me. Travelling to Montego Bay one Sunday, I kept reminding myself that I had never before in my life journeyed so many miles by car in one direction. There was more to Jamaica than its size, however. This country has a natural and diverse beauty which one can argue impressed me because of the limited exposure to the world I had had up till then. Almost fifty years later, however, having travelled throughout many regions of the world, I still maintain that Jamaica's natural beauty and diversity rank among the best internationally. In one relatively small (indeed very small) island as I now know it to be, one can find not only some of the most beautiful white sand beaches which, arguably, are to be found on any given Caribbean island, but also healing mineral springs, mountain lodges so high above sea level that one needs a fireplace to warm things up, and savannah regions rolling down to the sea. Portland with its majestic mountains and birthplace of the export trade in Jamaica bananas, western Jamaica with its rugged landscape and home of the Cockpit country where runaway slaves (Maroons) made their residence, and Westmoreland, the exact opposite of the powerful Portland parish – so green, so gentle and so peaceful before the reality of narcotics intruded.

There was industrial development too. I remember feeling a sense of regional pride for Jamaica's achievements when, in 1969, I saw factories which were actually producing goods which had always been associated with foreign manufacture. The mining of bauxite, albeit by foreign multinationals, was clearly evident and towns like Mandeville manifested the physical result of the wealth that the mining industry appeared to bring to the populace. The parish of Manchester prospered. Tourism was also on the upswing and sugar and banana production all seemed to be thriving. All told, Jamaica at the time gave the impression of being well ahead of the rest of the region, with greater ties to the United States than to the rest of the Caribbean, no doubt because of proximity, inter alia. The newly introduced Jamaica dollar was also higher in value than the US dollar!

What I failed to realize at the time has been aptly described in Dr. Eric Williams' flagship publication (1970), *From Columbus to Castro*, which I read several years later. According to Dr. Williams, the external control which the islands allowed over their natural and financial resources, whether oil, bauxite, sugar, tourism or finance (banking and insurance in particular) all signalled an inherent degree of fragmentation within the region which, to quote Williams, "goes to such fantastic lengths as would make the angels weep". Fragmentation in Jamaica was also evident at another level – racially and socially. The extent and depth of poverty manifested in the slums of Jamaica was new to me, as was the extreme wealth flaunted by the "haves" via their housing stock and the vehicles they drove.

Beverly Hills, the name reminiscent of California and Hollywood, posed no irony for its residents in its reflection of the foreign district after which it had obviously been named. Huge structures, one here shaped liked a crown, another there like a boat, all perched high on a Kingston mountain surveying their domain below – or so it seemed to me. But Beverly Hills was only one of many such enclaves, replicated several times over, particularly in the urban areas. The irony, however, was to be found at the very foothills or edges of these vast empires where, contrary to anything I had ever seen before or since in Trinidad, one could expect to find persons at the other end of the economic and social spectrum living in deep poverty and squalor. "Two Jamaicas" – so conspicuous even to my inexperienced and unsuspecting eye – subject of numerous articles and books and yet so completely normal to any Jamaican.

The concept of the "brown" Jamaican, too, I began to realize, was something not just real in this society, but a phenomenon to which extraordinary attention was paid and importance given. The brown Jamaican, while ethnically "black" is not dark-skinned in colour but rather is the beneficiary of a complexion that can range from spice brown to coffee loaded with milk. I was reminded of the time Frank and I were conversing with our Jamaican neighbours who lived in the flat upstairs ours in Trinidad and the notion of blackness came up, no doubt because we were discussing the subject of Black Power. Neville, a brown-skinned Jamaican, made it very clear in that conversation that he was not "black" but "brown" and we all laughed it off, little realizing how serious he must have been. Not surprisingly, colour was usually, though not always, related to class, job type and income level. But, beginning in the sixties in Jamaica, and in Trinidad and Tobago, the opening up of university education to a wide range of persons, especially those whose parents could not afford to send them overseas to acquire a college education, resulted in the relatively rapid rise of a black middle class, not just in the public but also in the private sector.

Everywhere unrest was simmering beneath the surface. The student unrest described earlier, which was taking place globally along with the Black Power Movement, was gaining a great deal of momentum in the region, particularly in Jamaica and Trinidad and Tobago. The New World Group, a liberal organization of Caribbean intellectuals receptive to left-leaning positions, had begun to flourish, particularly in Jamaica and Trinidad and Tobago. New World published a weekly newsletter named *Abeng* in Jamaica which, like *Moko* (started by James Millette as a deliberate move to the left) in Trinidad and Tobago, gave voice to the radical ideas expounded by this disgruntled political class. In similar fashion, the Rastafarian movement in Jamaica began to gain momentum rapidly and to spread to other parts of the Caribbean island chain.

Rastafarians, since the 1930s, had been questioning the inequalities in the society and had made no bones about trumpeting the fact that it was the Jamaican of unmistakable African lineage who was consistently relegated to the lower rungs of the society. A new social order was required and as this movement developed, it did so not merely along lines of principle and ethics, but also spirituality and culture as well. Rastafarians were more and more coming into their own, attracting in the process the young and the gifted. Thus, it was that in the mid to late sixties the songs of protest by artistes like Bob Marley and Peter Tosh were to be heard everywhere, with a consistent theme that the "people" should be freed from the shackles of "Babylon" – Babylon representing all that signified the oppression of black and working-class people in the society.

In 1968, Dr. Walter Rodney, a Guyanese lecturer in history at the Mona campus of UWI, on his return to Jamaica from Canada where he had gone to attend a conference, found himself unable to disembark the aircraft since in his absence he had been declared *persona non grata* and banned from re-entering the state. Rodney, an expert in African history, had been working among the Rastafarian community in Jamaica. Members of this community along with many of the university students objected to this action taken by the government and rioting ensued with casualties resulting. The mantle left by Rodney was assumed by a fellow lecturer, Dr. Clive Thomas also a Guyanese. Thomas spoke out clearly and unequivocally against the ban, in the process enunciating the radical ideas of the time relative to the governments of the Caribbean as lackeys who sought to place the interests of foreign investors before those of their own people. The Jamaican Government of the day, led by Mr. Hugh Shearer, in what might be called an unprecedented step, responded by banning Thomas as well, stoking even further the embers of political discontent in 1969.

It was impossible for me to ignore these events, the novelty of this situation of extremes which was now foisted on my consciousness. The issue was further compounded by my relationship with the university given Frank's association with it, now not as a freshman but a graduate student. This status allowed him to create relationships and expand his circle of interests and acquaintances to include somewhat radical elements which, the reader might recall, had for a long time been a particular interest of his.

The other side of the picture showed me a country and a people who were so delightful that I felt right at home in the society – warmth, hospitality and great food fuelling this delight in no uncertain terms. New friends were also made and former friends rediscovered. All of these persons helped to inject a sense of comfort and well-being into this new phase of my life and I was the happier for it. Frank loved driving and we had brought along our Austin 1100 motor vehicle. On weekends, we would often take off to explore places unknown. Sunday evenings were devoted to visiting friends.

One of Jamaica's peculiarities at that time was an openness of attitude which resulted in the norm of young women living on their own – not just campus students, but young women generally. In the Trinidad and Tobago society which I had left behind, it would have been considered scandalous for a young woman of "respectable origins" to move out of her family home and live on her own! Jamaica, on the other hand, was able to afford this privilege given the sophistication born of size, of proximity to her great northern neighbour and the fact of not being shackled by the bonds of Roman Catholicism which dominated Trinidadian society but had little impact on Jamaica. The size of the country also necessitated and thus developed a need for rural-based students to make use of boarding school facilities – a feature of academic life certainly unknown to the rest of the region! In the decades of the sixties and seventies, therefore, there were certainly signs of a strong feminist mentality and approach on the part of young women.

Liguanea and Papine were the shopping points, the former for things relatively sophisticated, and the latter for the down to earth stuff, especially fresh vegetables. Sophisticated Liguanea introduced me to the concept of the mall. Trinidad, in 1969, had no such facility which allowed persons to shop for a variety of items in one geographic space. Thus, in Liguanea, I could shop for food, have my hair cut, buy clothes, craft items, pharmaceuticals, you name it. Nor was it far from Mona Heights. Papine, on the other hand, also quite close to Mona Heights in the easterly direction, was the complete opposite. Papine was a village of the people – working class in every respect and with a Jamaican down-to-earthiness that could not be ignored. In a sense, both communities were a mirror image of Jamaican society.

I remember the Christmas Eve of 1971 when it suddenly dawned on me that there was no fresh pigeon peas (or gungo peas, the Jamaican name) to cook for the Christmas dinner. I rushed over to Papine and found one, solitary vendor with gungo peas, which were already shelled. Naturally, it had to be mine! But the vendor, to my surprise, said she couldn't sell it because it had been promised to someone who was coming back for it and she had agreed to hold it for her. Frantic at the prospect of eating a Christmas meal devoid of stewed green pigeon peas, I did something I had never done before nor since – I wheedled that poor woman into selling me the peas. Triumphant, I returned home with my trophy. But those peas had never been mine to enjoy – the vendor should have been allowed to keep them for the person to whom they had been promised. Cooking the peas in the traditional way, which by then I had been doing for three years, I placed a cup with water in the centre of the pot to keep hot and add to the peas as fast as the cooking water diminished. Well, the first time I opened the pot to add the water to the peas, the sight which met my eyes fairly reduced me to tears. There was the cup, all broken into many pieces lying among my precious peas. Staring in shock and in horror, I could only pick up the whole pot and dump its contents in the garbage. The moral of that story was quite clear to me.

My brother Reggie visited me during my first year in Jamaica and created, unwittingly no doubt, a sort of watershed in our sibling relationship such as it had been up to that point. The big brother I knew was always serious and uncommunicative, head usually buried in a book of some sort (one dared not look!) and, following the lead of my mother, it became common household practice to tiptoe around while in his presence and speak in whispers when speech became absolutely necessary. It was therefore with some trepidation that I greeted his arrival in Jamaica and the opportunity for the first time to meet and greet him on equal ground, so to speak, since we were now both adults.

He was staying with friends of his who invited Frank and me to have dinner with them one evening. There I was to acquaint myself for the first time with a side to my brother I never knew existed. The taciturn and detached person was transformed into a jovial and animated being who was the very life of the party! Moreover, as the evening wore on, his energy level and spirit only seemed to increase and it was with great reluctance that we finally made the move to say goodnight. Finally, I felt, I had a brother.

Introduction to the Rural Sector

The highlight of my Jamaica experience, however, was that of teaching. Scouring the newspaper one day shortly after my arrival on the island, my eyes fell on an advertisement indicating the need for a graduate teacher of Spanish and English at a school in Spanish Town. It was a Roman Catholic high school for girls only. I applied and was accepted for the position to teach the first, third and fifth forms. The first hurdle to be overcome was that of understanding what my students were saying. These were all rural children to whom the rich Jamaican Creole came naturally and while I marvelled at the beauty of the accents and the sounds which emerged from their mouths, it was also as important for me to understand what they were saying as it was for them to understand me. What a time!

Finally, I had a brainwave. I would give the third form a special project to collect current and original Jamaica sayings with a view to preparing a dictionary of Jamaican idioms and proverbs. Each week, each girl had to collect and orally present to the rest of the class at least five of these special words and phrases in the Jamaican creole followed by their transcription into Standard English. They would need to speak with grandparents and parents and jog each person's memory to come up with the most original of these sayings. The project was a roaring success. Not only did the students delve enthusiastically into the task of research and transcription, but I also learned a great deal that has not only remained with me up until today but also helped greatly in my understanding of the Jamaican culture and society.

"Rockstone a river bottom neva feel sun 'ot!"; "Sorry for magga dog, magga dag tun roun' bite yuh!"; "Play wid puppy, puppy lik yuh mout'"; "Doh close de stable door after de horse don gorn thru!" were some of my favourites. It made for a wonderful opportunity to help them learn Standard English which would make easier their understanding of the Spanish which I also had to teach them. But, more than the language and culture of Jamaica, my Spanish Town teaching experience brought to my subconscious an awareness of rural people – the needs, the realities, the challenges which they faced in their everyday lives, such as I had not experienced in Trinidad, owing no doubt to my naïveté and blinkered approach to life in general. I say subconscious because though I was aware that there were issues impacting on these rural girls, and while I empathized with them and did my part to help, like giving extra lessons after school, in retrospect, it was really a superficial (though concerned) reaction on my part. Later, I would recognize it for what it was – a serious developmental shortcoming in our Caribbean societies in general but with particularly negative impact on the rural communities.

Take, for example, the factor of rain in the rainy season. Those girls who lived in the Bog Walk and May Pen areas would be literally marooned in their homes and would have to wait, sometimes for days, while the flood waters subsided and the roads became passable before they could return to school – a fact of life accepted by all. Naturally this affected their studies since classes would continue for

*In Hope Gardens, Jamaica, picnicking (front row, 3rd right)
with my fifth formers now with exams behind them!*

those who were present, leaving the absentees to have to catch up as best they could with all of the subjects they were studying.

This was the early seventies and there was no question of technology assisting the absentee student. Moreover, these students had begun with a disadvantage. Having failed to secure places in the government school system, their parents were paying hard-earned money for them to attend this private secondary school. It was, however, a joy to teach those girls. They were not a brilliant lot but they received high marks for effort, in my view more encouraging to a teacher than natural brilliance which often leads to laissez-faire attitudes. Some seven years later, I would have the distinct pleasure of meeting one of the former third form students, studying law at the Cave Hill campus of the University of the West Indies.

And then Came Motherhood...

My first child was born in September of 1971. Due at the end of August, he chose to arrive some three weeks after he was expected and only after much nudging by the doctors – a procedure called induced labour which no one had hinted to me even existed. Indeed, no one had bothered either to tell me anything relative to the process of giving birth, inclusive of labour. By mid-September I was tired of being visited by former students and friends who had come to see the baby but instead encountered my more and more frustrated and still pregnant self. The fact that by then I had gained an extra forty pounds which sat awkwardly on my small frame, did nothing to improve my mood. So, one fine morning I packed my things, went to see the campus doctor and told him that I was not going back to the house unless I had the baby with me. He would have to admit me that very day to the University Hospital of the West Indies at Mona where I was scheduled for delivery. The doctor, Dr. Dyer, attempted, unsuccessfully, to reason with me by pointing out that in any event nothing could be done before the next morning. That was also fine by me. I was simply not going back to that house without a baby.

The baby, a boy, was finally born – clearly postmature judging from his dry and excessively wrinkled skin, and armed with a strong set of lungs which he never hesitated to use, usually for no particular reason. What changes such a tiny being could make to one's existence! Young families really ought to be warned to plan ahead so that the requisite lifestyle changes can be put in place to avoid the stress that will ultimately result unless there is planning and action in advance of the event! All I had really done, in retrospect, was to read my copy of Dr. Benjamin Spock's well-known book on which I relied to give me clues as to how to care for the baby once it arrived. Little did I know that there is much more to child rearing and family life than this.

There were other challenges too. Frank had completed his master's degree and was preparing himself to move on to the doctoral degree for which he would study in Geneva, Switzerland. In the interim he had secured a job as a research assistant at the Institute of Social and Economic Research (ISER), UWI which permitted him to broaden the scope of his research on the history of the Jamaican tourist industry.

In Geneva, he planned to pursue doctoral studies in the field of international politics at the Graduate Institute of International Studies. This institute, with a relatively small student body coming in the main from different parts of the world, was then as now, considered one of the world's most prestigious institutions. Standards set by the Institute for granting doctoral theses are very high. Impressed as I was by all of this, however, the very idea of moving so far out of my geographic and language range, to live in a country whose people neither looked like me nor spoke the way I did, struck terror into my unsophisticated self.

I proposed to Frank that he follow his dream whereas I, meanwhile, would move back to Trinidad with the baby, Frank Ayodele, and continue to teach. Those rural Jamaican girls obviously had inspired me to think that I had finally hit on a career choice. There was no fear in my mind as to how I would now manage as a single mother and career woman. I had been raised by a woman who had subtly taught me by example all I needed to know; I was all ready now to continue with my teaching, having secured three years of combined experience between Trinidad and Jamaica and no teenager, never mind how much taller or stronger, could intimidate me. But Frank would have none of it – either his family accompanied him or no one would be going.

Hindering his dream in any way was the last thing I wanted to do. Nor could I morally do it. Simply put, this man, from the outset of our relationship, had outlined his dreams and ambitions for himself. By marrying him I too had bought into the dream and become a voluntary and legitimate part of the system of values he had established for himself long before I met him. And so, still disinclined to make the move, I nonetheless shouldered my moral responsibility and agreed to begin the process by which we would accompany him. But how were we to survive? We were now a family of three and although there was the expectation that he would gain scholarship support, surely this would not suffice to take care of books, food, clothing (now for four seasons of the year) and shelter. If I could not teach in Geneva, for obvious reasons, then what would I do?

I then wrote to my brother, by that time a career diplomat, to seek his advice and possible help since he too had, some years earlier, studied and lived in Geneva. Reggie found out that there was an opening for a position of clerk/typist at the Trinidad and Tobago Mission to the United Nations which was based in Geneva. It was what was called a locally recruited position for which anyone could apply and over which the local mission had complete jurisdiction in the selection of the candidate. I applied for and was accepted for the position. But clerk/typist? The clerical aspect I could handle but I had never been even five feet close to a typewriter. The answer was clear: I would have to sign up for a course in typewriting. For three months, I attended the Fitz-Henley School of Typing and Commerce in Kingston, Jamaica and left with a certificate which said that I could type. I was now fully qualified for the job – a job which, as it turned out, never for one single moment required me to type even a single letter of the alphabet.

It was with a degree of reluctance that I left Jamaica at the time I did since politically it was an exciting period. Michael Manley had just succeeded Hugh Shearer as Prime Minister and his charisma and the promise that his leadership held for the country were unquestionable. Manley had campaigned with a symbolic "Rod of Correction", and accompanied by reggae songs and slogans which allowed no guessing as to their meaning. "Let the Power Fall on I", "Better Mus' Come", "Dey Mus' Get a Beatin'" were some of the more popular songs and slogans around. And the population readily rallied. Perhaps the proclamations and utterances of Rodney and Thomas had left their mark, or maybe the populace had merely tired of an administration led by a Prime Minister, Hugh Shearer, whose name had been punned "Share Out". Or perhaps it was that global events and movements of students and of Black Power had cheered the people on. Whatever the reason or reasons, Michael Manley was swept to power in an undeniable victory.

My sojourn in Jamaica was now over and as I courageously turned my sights towards Geneva, Switzerland, I could hardly guess that my Jamaican rural teaching experience would be brought to bear on a level of consciousness I would develop in this most unlikely of places, changing the entire course of my life and my thinking. Little did I know either that the political victory of Michael Manley and the PNP would return to have an impact on me outside of the boundaries of this state and in the context of a Grenada Revolution which no one at the time could have predicted.

Frank, as it turned out, would prevail. By the end of the four-year period which he set himself he had completed and successfully presented his PhD thesis on Cuba, in the context of international relations, from its 1959 revolutionary period.

4 ✌ Geneva, Switzerland 1972-1976

WE AGREED THAT we would travel to Switzerland via New York and London, mainly to visit relatives we were not certain to see again anytime soon, Switzerland appearing to be such a far-off country. In New York I marvelled at the height of the buildings which made London's Post Office Tower look small by comparison. That particular building had really impressed me on a visit to England two years earlier to attend my sister Marina's wedding. And, as had happened on my visit there, I wondered at the brilliance of human beings who could create intricate and extended rail systems which ran below the ground, seemingly without a hitch.

From New York we travelled to London, and stayed with Marina and her husband, Lionel. The contrast was remarkable in some ways. The weather was certainly colder there and gave a preview of things to come, useful, since I had never experienced cold weather. To make matters worse, central heating in the early seventies was hardly commonplace in London and many people relied instead on individual heating units in the various rooms. No doubt residents of England were used to this and acclimatized accordingly. Certainly, we were not. Was this what we were to look forward to in Geneva? Frank, historian as he was, wondered at the progress of a country which had once "ruled the waves", spearheaded the Industrial Revolution, played a major role in the colonization of the New World, of Africa and of Asia. Wasn't it reasonable to expect to see more concrete results of this former glory?

Our visit to London coincided with an event of international proportions which, although it did not affect us directly, nevertheless fairly dominated our time there. It was the summer of 1972, the time of the Munich Olympic Games. Towards the end of the Games, Palestinian members of the Black September Movement, the most extremist of the Palestinian groups, took a number of Israeli athletes hostage in an effort to dramatically bring the Palestinian question to the attention of the rest of the world. It all ended tragically with the hostages being killed and their Palestinian captors as well, cut down by bullets from German sharpshooters.

Finally, the day came when we were to travel to Switzerland. But it was not to go by without hitches and hurdles. First, the laid-back Frank convinced Lionel, the resident of London, that the originally allocated time for getting to the airport was excessive. We could do it in much shorter time. Lionel, equally laid-back, went along with the plan. Well, the traffic turned out to be so horrendous that we lost the flight, which left us completely stranded since Peter, one of Frank's "group of five" from St. Augustine, was scheduled to meet us and take us to the apartment which he had secured for our rental. Mobile phones were non-existent at the time and we had no way of reaching Peter by landline.

Finally, we were put on a later flight to Geneva and, several hours later, tired, bewildered, and with a very irritable baby in tow, we arrived at our destination. There had been reference by someone of our acquaintance of Switzerland being a "police state", a reference which had been shrugged off as unimportant and immaterial to our purposes. The reality of the reference was, however, brought fully to life on our arrival. Processing of our papers, credentials and identities seemed to take forever and no one was in any particular hurry to short-circuit a process which was standard practice. At long last we were outside of the immigration and customs areas and looked around hopefully as if expecting that Peter, by some magical influence, would be there waiting. But we were entirely on our own, in a country we had never visited, to whose now cold weather we were unaccustomed, whose language we did not speak fluently, and unaware of where we were going to stay.

As luck would have it, Reggie had given me a list of contacts, friends of his in Geneva, on whom we could call in the event that we needed some assistance. I happened to have the list handy and we called the first person on the list. No one answered so we called the second number which was answered by a gentleman who, as soon as he heard reference to Reggie, immediately abandoned his Sunday afternoon gardening and, without even bothering to change into street clothes, came immediately to fetch us. Not only was his English perfect (which after the day I had had plus the additional stress of having to deal with immigration and customs was an unquestionable relief) but he also turned out to be a senior professor at the Institut des Hautes Etudes Internationales where Frank would be studying. And, as if all of this were not enough, he was a member of the board of directors which supervised the student residence attached to the Institute. We were home free! There could not possibly have been a better ending to what had been one of the longest and most traumatic days of my life. And he did not leave until he ensured that we were checked in and fully comfortable in our one-bedroom modern furnished apartment, the monthly rental of which was affordable.

Our extremely compact accommodation was the last word in comfort and style. It was the tiniest kitchen I had ever seen but no facility seemed to be missing from it. There were cupboards above and below the sink, a four-burner stove with an oven, a fridge, sink and drain board. All these conveniences were located along one side of the passageway which led in and out of the apartment and did not take up more than five feet of space. The bedroom furniture comprised a double bed, in the entire bottom section of which were drawers for storage of linen and blankets. The clothes cupboard had space not only for hanging but upper cupboards for more storage, shelves on the side and drawers at the bottom. The living area had two easy chairs made of leatherette and chrome, shelving for books, music and the like and a dining table and two straight-backed chairs. And, there was central heating!

Ah, Switzerland!

Such a profusion of life-changing memories and experiences. Switzerland had been set up as a buffer state in Europe following the Napoleonic Wars with the idea that it would be a neutral state bordering on the countries of Germany, France and Italy. It took its neutrality very seriously. What I had not known before I arrived was that there are three official language zones, depending on the country with which it shares a border. Thus, there is French Switzerland – Suisse Romande – which is French-speaking and shares a border with France; German Switzerland which shares a border with Germany and where Swiss German is spoken; and Italian Switzerland sharing a border with Italy and where Swiss Italian is spoken. It appears that over time these various languages have evolved and while one can easily converse with someone who speaks the original language, Switzerland's three native languages are ultimately peculiar to herself.

This characteristic of neutrality made Switzerland the perfect location for establishing a seat of the United Nations with Missions from throughout the world accredited to it, Trinidad and Tobago among them. Exceedingly wealthy, with what was said to be the highest per capita income in the world and zero unemployment at the time I was there, the Swiss managed their country and economy with a discipline that was admirable. Citizenship issues were clear. The children of a Swiss father were automatically entitled to Swiss nationality. But this rule did not automatically apply if the mother of the children was Swiss but the father non-Swiss, even if these children were born in Switzerland. Such children could acquire Swiss nationality but only after applying for it on attaining the age of 18. Children born in Switzerland of non-Swiss parents had no entitlement in this regard. Thus, it was that years later, we constantly struggled to impress upon our daughter Janine Omolara, who learned to speak fluently before she was a year old and loved to strike up conversations with strangers, that she should refrain from telling people that she was Swiss, but rather a Trinidadian born in Switzerland.

Almost the first thing that struck me about the society was the sense of orderliness. All the buildings looked clean and tidy, the buses ran on time, the many parks were all neatly kept. Even the weather did its part. Geneva was consistently cold except for a few weeks at the height of summertime. You could set your watch by the expected arrival of the buses whose drivers were known to slow down the speed of the bus if it threatened to arrive even a few minutes ahead of the set schedule. I took the bus to work for the first year of my stay there and standing at the bus stop on the edge of the beautiful Geneva Lake (*le lac de Genève*) which dominates the city with its famous water fountain (*le jet d'eau*) would have been a fabulous experience were it not for that north wind (*la bise*). Consistently it made its presence known and felt, its coldness penetrating, it seemed, even to the very marrow of my bones.

Geneva charmed me with its sense of agelessness, of antiquity so perfectly preserved that it seemed like the sophisticated norm to be expected from a society such as this. One therefore grew accustomed to floors constructed of marble, to gold lettering in high relief – without any characters missing – which identified the names of buildings. Elevators had brass handrails, carpeted floors, smoked glass doors and porters who took their job very seriously, from the way they wore their uniforms to the measured steps with which they walked.

One would almost believe they were acting out a role in a play.

In the seventies, to be a black person in Geneva usually meant that you were either a diplomat or a student. Immigrant workers tended to be drawn from Italy or Spain and so, while there was a certain reserve on the part of the Swiss towards people of colour, there was also a great deal of respect shown. Exceedingly polite but not at all what one would call warm, the Swiss would virtually go out of their way to assist once assistance was requested. One was, however, expected to observe the unwritten and unspoken rules of the society. One African student recounted that he had committed the unforgiveable sin of taking a newspaper from the little boxes in which they were regularly placed without putting the requisite coin in the adjoining box located there for the purpose of receiving payment for newspapers taken. No one ever monitored the sale of the newspapers for it was the expectation, indeed the custom, that if you helped yourself to a newspaper, you paid for it. His action had been observed by an elderly woman who reprimanded him severely for what he had done (or failed to do) and when the bus came along, right on time as usual, she followed him on to the bus and continued her lecture. He never did it again.

Yet another student, Dutch this time, while relaxing in one of Geneva's beautiful parks, unwrapped a candy bar and flicked the wrapper on to the grass. He shortly thereafter became aware of a little old lady hobbling across to where the wrapper had been dropped. Reaching the spot, she bent down painfully, retrieved the wrapper and deliberately placed it in one of the bins which had been provided for the purpose. He, too, never repeated the error and, indeed, found himself unable to stay in the park any longer.

One got the impression that there was this collective sense of community responsibility on the part of the citizens for the role they played in the development and maintenance of the country. It was as if the state were an enterprise and they the shareholders. As time went by, I was to witness more of what to me was remarkable behaviour, even by children. I lived for three of the four years which I spent in Geneva on the third floor of a multi-story apartment building. The ground floor of an adjacent building comprised a supermarket. The supermarket opened at 8 a.m. but suppliers, from as early as 6.30 a.m. would begin to deliver their merchandise and, since the store was closed, they would leave the items outside. I am talking about crates of apples and other fruit, loaves of bread – items which, individually, anyone can easily make off with, particularly the school children who passed there in droves each morning on their way to school, chattering with each other. Morning after morning I watched from my third-floor window, expecting to witness the potential offense committed by the child who would finally be tempted to grab an apple or pinch at a loaf of bread. But my wait was in vain – those children did not even look in the direction of the items lined up outside of a closed and locked supermarket. They simply passed them by.

The housewives were another source of interest to me and I had a good opportunity to observe them while I was on maternity leave after the birth of my daughter. They woke early – this was the first thing that struck me – and immediately the chores began. Observing the goings-on on the various floors of the apartment complex across from mine, I could see these women opening their windows and airing the bed linen no doubt while preparing children for school or to accompany their mother while she shopped. Not long thereafter, they would appear on the street, well-coiffed with children in stroller or held by one hand, shopping bag in the next.

It was therefore no surprise to me that the Swiss, who vote on all matters pertaining to the conduct of their separate cantons or states (at least at the time I was there), voted in 1976 against adopting a shortened version of the work week which was being proposed as an alternative to what was then in force. A wealthy country yes, but one comprising a people who daily earned the privilege of enjoying this wealth.

There were many early adjustments to be made to the thinking to which I had grown accustomed, to my former casual manner of dress, to having the full responsibility of a child without any maternal or domestic support, to living in a student residence with nationalities from all over the world, to now having to utilize the metric as against the imperial system of weights and measures. Then there was the language. I discovered that the French done in school and studied at university in the Caribbean is not the French spoken by the Swiss. Thus, what I had thought to be in my favour by way of a head start to settling into this new life and community turned out to be yet another challenge. Not that I was fluent in French, mind you, but certainly I knew enough to understand and make myself understood.

Subconsciously, all these happenings and observations on my

part regarding a society in which I knew I could not spend the rest of my life, but which I respected greatly, were having an impact on me. I recollect feeling a sense of wonderment at fellow West Indians who had, for whatever reason, travelled to that part of the world, a world which formed no cultural or historical association for them – yet they had stayed! They had settled into the society, married and borne children who would not necessarily know or understand anything about 50% of their own roots. I realize now that to my young and uninformed mind the word "migration" held no meaning for me. All I could think of was the fact that they were not giving back to their parent societies; that perhaps they were giving up on the experiences and history of their forefathers – and wondered how they thought they could ever really belong? I am still unsure of whether I have managed to resolve that dilemma within myself.

Trinidad Re-visited

I found myself comparing Switzerland with Trinidad and Tobago and concluding that there were a couple of key similarities. Switzerland, by European standards, is a small country – like Trinidad and Tobago. It is also a wealthy country – like Trinidad and Tobago. There ended the comparison, however, for while the Swiss took the business of their long-term development very seriously and demonstrated people participation in the process, I could hardly say the same for my country.

This was demonstrated in no uncertain terms when, some three years after arriving in Switzerland, I travelled back to Trinidad to spend some time with my mother. Nothing had prepared me for what I found. In the mere six years since I had lived there the economy had experienced an economic boom as a result of the 1973 oil crisis – a crisis which had precipitated not merely a huge increase in the price of petroleum but changes in the control of the commodity at the national level. Shell, Texaco and others had been banished and replaced in 1974 and 1975 by state-owned Trintoc and Trintopec which, in turn, had their interests consolidated with the incorporation in 1993 of state-owned Petrotrin. "Money is no problem" became the rallying cry of the Prime Minister and his Government – and this was no idle boast. Instances of the impact and effect of this boom were everywhere. All my former friends now boasted (and I mean "boasted") two cars and fancy homes in which they lived. Some of them had actually become entrepreneurs (I had known none when I left) of hardware stores and construction companies and everyone was talking about making their first million. The only person, it seemed to me, who had not changed and was carrying on as she had always done was my mother. She continued to complain about the cost of everything and to consider carefully the cost of anything before she purchased it.

It would be an experience that would strike me with particular force and demonstrate to me beyond a doubt the change that had taken place in the psyche and mores of the society when one day I took a taxi to travel into Port of Spain. I had been used to a custom whereby the passenger, on entering a taxi with a twenty-dollar bill, needed to advise the driver accordingly so that he could stop, usually at a gas station and make change – the fare being in the region of four dollars. So, armed with my twenty-dollar bill, I advised my driver accordingly. He didn't stop anywhere to make change, however, and I had the shock of my life when, on arriving in Port of Spain, every single one of the other four passengers handed him a one-hundred-dollar bill and he made change for every last one without blinking an eye. Needless to say, not only did I spend the morning in a state of shock, but also that this experience captured in a nutshell for me, how the society had changed excessively in a very short space of time. Money really seemed to be no problem.

The other observation which alarmed me and brought me to a conclusion which was to have a major impact on my life (although at the time I did not realize it) was the change which had occurred in the spirit of the average Trinidadian. Perhaps I was affected because my former close interaction with those rural children from Jamaica whose lifestyles, so simple yet so full of effort and meaning, had made an impression somewhere deep inside me. Or perhaps it was the stark contrast between my own country, newly rich and small, with the other, also small but wise in the use of its long-standing wealth. The piles of garbage in Trinidad, everywhere it seemed, were but symbolic of our newfound ability to purchase multiple packaged and imported goods, and served only to remind me of Swiss pride in their surroundings, including public thoroughfares.

Sad but true, I became suddenly aware of our propensity to indiscriminately slash and burn the vegetation on our hills and to use our rivers, beaches and drains as our personal dumping ground. The feeling that as a people we no longer cared for each other and treated our human and physical resources accordingly made my mind hark back to a busy city street where a stranger approached would stop and take time to give directions to someone who was clearly a stranger in their midst, and an arthritic old lady would pick up a single candy wrapper dropped by someone else and place it in its designated location. Did I really want to raise my children here? I didn't think so.

My Introduction to Development Theory

But, what might have created the greatest impact of all on me was my job, which I had secured in 1973 at the World Council of Churches (WCC). A miniature United Nations but with a spiritual approach and emphasis, the WCC was at the time headed by Dr. Phillip Potter, a Dominican. Amazing but true, the tiny, under-populated Caribbean island of Dominica had produced a son of the soil who had risen to assume the helm of this all-important organization. There were other highly placed West Indians there too – Dame Nita Barrow of Barbados and Dr. Roy Neehall of Trinidad and Tobago among them.

It was by chance that I had happened upon this institution. Tired of hearing me complain of my life of sheer boredom at the Trinidad and Tobago Mission, a friend one day casually suggested that I apply to the World Council of Churches to see if there was anything available. I dropped off my application one morning on the way to work at the Mission and, as I was stepping through the main door, the phone was ringing for me. Dr. Julio de Santa Ana, the person who was to have the greatest intellectual impact on my life, had just seen my application and résumé and was calling to invite me to interview for a job. What had clinched things for me was the fact that my mother tongue was English and I had a degree in Spanish and French – a combination which in the mid-seventies was exceedingly rare in Geneva.

My job was to translate into English, from the Spanish and French languages in which he wrote, the papers of Prof. de Santa Ana, former political prisoner, Uruguayan exile, Christian-Marxist theologian and intellectual. As I translated, I learned and as I learned more and more from Julio about a world and a development approach to life that I could never have imagined existed, my fascination grew and grew. Development, I learned, was not so much about infrastructure – roads, bridges and buildings, and so on – as much as it is about people. True development cannot be achieved without the participation of the people involved; after this would come the infrastructural and other aspects of development, I found in later experiences, to be the key to a real understanding of development.

The WCC department in which I had found myself was something of an experiment for the organization. It was called the Commission for the Churches' Participation in Development (CCPD) and had been recently established with a view to determining ways in which the churches throughout the world could become significantly involved in the development of their communities. Working as he did for the Latin American and Caribbean section, Julio's work and writings introduced me to a world which, while geographically so close, I had been completely unaware of until then.

The development of my social ideas had begun in earnest. The principles of "liberation theology" had been introduced at the Latin American Archbishops' Conference in Medellin, Colombia in 1968. Briefly, it postulated that biblical references needed to be applied to everyday happenings, particularly to the populations of the developing world, with a view to providing concrete and responsible responses. Thus, it was that the system of apartheid, of corruption in government, of amassing weapons of mass destruction, of transnationals and their rape of the economies of developing countries, of desertification and famine in countries like Ethiopia – issues such as these all had to be viewed in theological terms as being against the will of God and thus sinful within the biblical context. In socio-economic terms, they were simply unjust. Responses thus needed to be provided in developmental terms with the interests of the people at heart. Countries of whose existence I had been unaware now began to appear on my radar and to assume significance and stature in terms of their peoples and their problems.

I was reminded of this forty years later in November 2014 when the Pontiff, His Holiness Pope Francis, addressed the European parliament. His was a message to the leaders that their confidence be restored in man, "not so much as a citizen or an economic agent, but in man, in men and women as persons endowed with transcendent dignity". He urged his audience to keep alive not merely democracies, but also human and environmental ecology along with an investment in individuals, all as a means of manifesting the political will of the people. Failing this, he warned, democracies would collapse "under the pressure of multilateral interests which are not universal, which weaken them and turn them into uniform systems of economic power at the service of unseen empires...."

Not much had changed from the message of the CCPD, it seemed.

Acquaintance with far-off places was not limited to talk and thought. The opportunity to travel to places I would not ordinarily have visited also emerged. Thus, it was that I travelled to the then Soviet Union as a member of a CCPD team who were guests of the Russian Orthodox Church. The very notion of church in the context of the Soviet Union in the mid-seventies was both peculiar and exciting. We travelled to Moscow and then to a monastery town called Zagorsk. In Moscow, we viewed the remains of Lenin and dined on seven-course meals. I had never suspected that such a practice existed. It was also the first time that I was sampling both the vodka and the caviar native to Russia and which were so proudly and so frequently served to us. We even had sturgeon one evening but this was casually waved off by our hosts who jokingly told us that this was the part of the fish they normally threw away, once the eggs or the caviar had been removed!

Still relatively politically and socially immature at that stage, I was nonetheless struck by the shabby clusters of multi-apartment buildings, all bearing several tall antennae which dominated the landscape. It was clear that these multiple antennae were meant to ensure that the continuously televised messages of the government were efficiently received by the Soviet people, their tatty housing notwithstanding. It was a sight which seemed to me incongruous with the notion of this country as a global super power. The surprise (or maybe it should not have been) came later when we were shown the wooded retreats and dachas of the hierarchy, making me wonder at a system which claimed to be run on the basis of equality and services for all.

In Zagorsk – so named during Soviet times but now restored to its original name Sergiyev Posad – we stayed at the monastery, a far cry from the splendour of the hotel in which we resided while in Moscow. Sergiyev Posad is famed for the 14th century Trinity Lavra St. Sergius monastery complex, and as the spiritual centre of the Russian Orthodox Church. Under early communism the Church's property was nationalized and many of the clergy jailed and killed. In response, parts of the Church made themselves into pro-Soviet types of churches in order to survive. However, when Hitler's forces invaded and almost succeeded in conquering the country, Stalin had to turn to the Orthodox and other churches for support in return for which the Soviet government granted these churches limited freedom of existence and activity.

In Zagorsk, some of the monks actually gave up their rooms to accommodate us and we now dined on meals which were as simple yet as adequate as our sleeping accommodation. The real surprise for me was the great splendour of the Russian Orthodox cathedral in contrast to all other surroundings. It matched the gorgeous trappings associated with the Roman Catholic Church not merely by way of the pomp and ceremony of the service but also in the ornamental accessories and the vestments of the officiating priests.

It was interesting too to analyse the composition of the congregation which comprised mainly old people (the majority of whom were women) and children. The church was packed to capacity however, as it happened to be the time of one of the Church festivals. Not many years later, resident in Grenada and travelling once more to the Soviet Union before its breakup into separate nation states, this time as a guest of the government, a completely different picture of the role and status of the Church was painted. Our guide pointed out buildings which were shuttered and closed, which she said were churches that were hardly used anymore. Each time she said this, an image of my 1975 Zagorsk experience would come to mind and I would shake my head in disbelief, knowing with some sense of certainty that despite the official communiqués, the Russian Orthodox Church continued to prevail in the lives of many Soviet citizens.

Slowly but surely, the strands of my life experiences, of exposure to radical thought and ideas, began to take shape and form and by 1975, the mosaic had begun to sharpen itself on my consciousness. I realized that step by step, from my childhood upbringing, to exchanges of progressive ideas over time with the one who was now my husband and father of my son and daughter, to teacher and mentor of children from a rural and unworldly-wise context, I had become subtly immersed into an atmosphere of ideological sophistication and development praxis entirely removed from anything I had ever experienced. A new me was beginning to emerge. It was difficult to ignore the very irony of the fact that an environment which was, by definition, so alien to my earlier experiences would offer the opportunity for the crafting and moulding of the social conscience which began to take shape within me, in the process spawning a growing self-radicalization. I would never look back.

My outlook on life began to assume a completely different

trajectory and I could ignore none of it. Work in the field of NGOs and development programming was clearly the way I had to go on my return to the Caribbean. I did not immediately cast aside the prospect of teaching once again but it assumed a rather dim appearance on the horizon of my future. What was strange, however, was that although I knew what I wanted to do, it was difficult for me to picture myself in the particular situation, given that living in the Caribbean had not exposed me in any way to this new approach to life and work. I had taught children from disadvantaged homes and communities, but not met their families nor acquainted myself in any acute fashion with their lifestyle. I had lived in the Caribbean, totally unconscious of the need to contribute except to the immediate family to which I belonged. Nor had I even been aware of the concept of community participation and development. My experience with the World Council of Churches in Geneva introduced me to the theory of this new concept of development. But how was I to put it into practice?

In 1976 Frank completed and successfully presented his PhD thesis and the family began preparations for a return to the Caribbean. As for where we should go, ultimately that proved to be Barbados. Jamaica, beloved Jamaica, was our first preference but there were no openings in the history department. Trinidad, given the situation outlined earlier in this chapter, was out of the question. This left us with Cave Hill, Barbados, a country hitherto unknown to us but which bore a certain appeal since my sister, Marina, had returned to the region and was living there along with her spouse whose father's roots were Barbadian. As luck would have it, a position opened up in the Department of History at the Cave Hill campus just when Frank was about to apply for a position at UWI and it readily became his.

Barbados also happened to be one of the islands where a main office of the Caribbean Conference of Churches (CCC), a sister organization of the WCC, was located. This created some excited anticipation on my part at the potential opportunity to work with this organization and put into action what were for me, up until then, mere theories and ideas. Perhaps now there could be the opportunity to invest by way of committed action and in a Caribbean context with which I was familiar and to which I felt I belonged.

Little did I suspect what really lay in store for me!

150, ROUTE DE FERNEY   P.O. BOX No. 66   1211 GENEVA 20   ●   TELEPHONE : (022) 33 34 00   ●   TELEX : 23 423 OIK CH   ●   CABLE : OIKOUMENE GENEVA

WORLD COUNCIL OF CHURCHES

PROGRAMME UNIT ON JUSTICE AND SERVICE
Commission on the Churches' Participation in Development

A QUIEN CORRESPONDA

Por la presente dejamos constancia que la Sra. Regina Taylor cumplió
tareas de Secretaria del Coordinador de Estudios de la Comisión para
la Participación de las Iglesias en el Desarrollo, del Consejo Mundial
de Iglesias. A tal efecto tuvo a su cargo la administración de dicho
sector, manteniendo al día la correspondencia (en inglés, español y
francés), el servicio de documentación de esa oficina, y encargáse de
los detalles prácticos relativos a la organización de varios encuentros
y conferencias internacionales. También tuvo bajo su responsabilidad
la traducción al inglés de textos escritos en español y/o francés,
así como también la edición de los mismos. Todos estos trabajos fueron
cumplidos a entera satisfacción por la Sra. Regina Taylor, quien
demostró un alto grado de capacitación y dinamismo en la realización de
las tareas que le fueran adjudicadas.

En Ginebra, el 2 de febrero de 1977

Julio de Santa Ana
Coordinador de Estudios
Comisión para la Participación de
las Iglesias en el Desarrollo

JSA/eh

*Letter written by my mentor, Julio de Santa Ana, on my departure from the
World Conference of Churches*

5 🌿 Barbados 1976-1980: I Meet "Little England"

I SWORE I WOULD never drive in Barbados. After four years of auto routes and international highways, nothing had prepared me for the narrow motorways of Barbados. It seemed to me impossible that the streets could contain two vehicles going in opposite directions. Moreover, the Barbadian practice of vehicles going in separate directions stopping abreast of each other so that the drivers could have a chat really was the last straw.

Barbadian society failed to reflect the warmth which, particularly based on my Jamaica experience, I had taken for granted as a characteristic of any Caribbean island. Indeed, it was akin to living in Geneva but in a context of black faces and warm weather. People were polite but not warm; colleagues were pleasant to you at work but never invited you to their homes. If the occasion warranted that you visit their home you were expected to call ahead. But the unkindest cut of all was that if you were not Barbadian you were referred to as a "foreigner". Without the presence of my sister I am not sure how long I could have stayed in Barbados. My family and I were, however, frequent visitors to her home, where I met Barbadians through her husband's family connections and little by little began to feel more at home with both the Barbadian accent and the society at large.

As a family, we continued to make efforts to take a drive on the odd Sunday afternoon but this was a country two and a half times smaller than Trinidad, so one quickly ran out of options. One was not even allowed the challenge and adventure of getting lost and finding one's way back, since the Barbadian authorities had helpfully placed signs on all the bus stops (and there are many in Barbados) indicating whether one is heading to the city or from the city. The beaches were available but held no attraction for a non-swimmer who had come close to drowning as a child. Gone was the enticing quality of a moonlight dip at Carenage Bay – with two young children the notion of spontaneity was replaced by a sense of responsibility and since every Barbadian seemed as good a swimmer as Frank, I was relegated the task of sitting on the beach and guarding the towels.

In retrospect, I made no Barbadian friends in Barbados. Andrea, Marina's sister-in-law, and I had become such fast friends when we met in England in 1970 for the wedding of our respective siblings, that the following year when my son was born, she was declared the godmother. It was therefore a great pleasure to be reunited with her now in Barbados. However, apart from her, my friends were either old acquaintances from Trinidad whom I was really pleased to meet again or a couple of new ones, also from Trinidad. I remember saying once to my Barbadian boss, with whom I got along really well, "How come you have never invited me and my family to your home?" Clearly taken aback by the question, he laughed and finally said, "Well, it never occurred to me, really...."

And therein lay the difference between Barbados and, say, Trinidad or certainly Jamaica. Trinidadians, as a matter of course, would have made it a point to invite the visitor, the new arrival, to their homes, even if only once. Judging from the response given by Lambert, my boss, that sort of requirement to be hospitable was simply not an issue – it had never occurred to him, he said. Not that putting the idea in his mind helped any, since we still never were invited by him or any of the other Barbadian colleagues.

Barbados is fondly called "Little England" by its citizens and proud of this nickname they are. The island of Barbados is quite pretty with many white sand beaches scattered along its western and southern coasts. A large measure of the island's charm lies in the beautifully restored and maintained plantation houses which have become part of the Barbados National Trust and, indeed, its geographic landscape. Several of the Caribbean islands have established National Trusts over the years but Barbados, Jamaica, and possibly St. Lucia have taken the notion more seriously than the others. The cultivation of sugarcane (with rum produced as a by-product) was still an important income earner in the later seventies when I was there. While the sugar estates with their factories dating back hundreds of years exuded a mixture of beauty and charm at a physical level, there was nonetheless, blended with this a sense of revulsion and aversion given the brutal history associated with sugar production in the region. Exceedingly flat in the main, the landscape held little attraction for a lover of mountains and valleys as I am. And, of course, rivers were out of the question.

The flat nature of Barbados' topography, in addition to its small size, was brought sharply home to me once when I was on a plane which was about to land in Barbados. The captain, speaking to the passengers advised that those seated on the left-hand side of the aircraft would be able to get a good view of the western portion of Barbados. He hesitated and then added, "Well, all of Barbados, really...."

I arrived in Barbados at a time when the government had started to take a close look at tourism and to take the industry really seriously. Those of us from other countries in the region who have lived and worked in Barbados would be aware that Barbadians do more than pay lip service to issues which they identify as priority. Tourism had never impacted on me, growing up as I did in Trinidad where the tourist dollar had not been sought after and where visitors – when we saw them in Port of Spain, clad in Bermuda shorts, colourful shirts and straw hats – were merely to be giggled at and tolerated. The island of Tobago, rather, was the locus of the country's overtures to tourism. Jamaica, on the other hand, had been actively encouraging and promoting tourism since the late nineteenth century, but it appeared to be more enclave tourism confined to its north coast. Before 1919 it was Port Antonio that was the centre of tourism development in Jamaica. By 1939 Montego Bay had emerged and after 1970, Westmoreland. In Jamaica, I had lived on the edges of the university campus and worked in Spanish Town and so was shielded from the social fallout of the tourism phenomenon there as well.

In Barbados, however, no doubt because of its small size and the tremendous energy and other resources which the government poured into its development, one could not ignore tourism. It was supported by a campaign designed to penetrate every corner and sector of the society and this it did – from the schoolchild to the adult, from the private sector to the public, from the churches to the masses at large. Barbados boasted of sixty miles of coastline "a smile wide" – a slogan no doubt coined to elicit the cooperation of the public at large towards welcoming the visitor. One issue which struck me forcibly was that of access to the beaches by the public.

It was the practice of hotels located on the beaches there to offer their guests exclusive use of that strip of beach and, I daresay, the water which fronted the hotel. By exclusive, I mean just that. The local population was expected to utilize only those portions of beach located on the fringes of the hotels' beach front. And, as one might expect, these hotels were located in the main along the west and south coasts where the best beaches are to be found. For years, apparently, this had been a hot topic debated by politicians and population alike. That the government of the day proclaimed a policy change in this regard was therefore the climax to a long-awaited promise and, perhaps (and this is mere speculation on my part), a mechanism for engaging the populace in a campaign that could not possibly have succeeded without their key input and coop-eration. And, at least to my non-native Barbadian and untrained eye, it did.

Baxter's Road was perhaps what one might venture to include among the tourism specialties of Barbados. Situated close to the heart of the city of Bridgetown, Baxter's Road really only came alive at night. And what a liveliness it generated! Chief among the attrac-tions was the fish, usually mahi mahi, seasoned and fried to abso-lute perfection and served with breadfruit. The breadfruit merely represented the trappings, for it was the fish itself which was the attraction and was prepared while you waited and drooled with longing to bite into the tasty flesh once it had cooled. All around would be sounds of laughter, of cooking, of socializing generally.

As for the churches! Anglicanism prevailed and still does, but with a population of only 250,000 it seemed that Barbados was still able to accommodate several other denominations: Moravians, Roman Catholics, Methodists, Seventh Day Adventists, Pentecos-tals, and so on. Indeed, although I was not able to substantiate this, rumour had it that Barbados has the highest number of denomi-national churches per capita in the region and probably the world.

But How Was Regina Faring?

Neither fate, genetic considerations nor my newfound Geneva based consciousness would allow me the luxury of being a middle-class housewife to be cared for by her professional husband. An opportunity to teach in a girls' high school with a wonderful reputa-tion presented itself early on and while I still planned to pursue my plan to seek employment at the Caribbean Conference of Churches, I readily jumped at the opportunity, hoping to replicate, no doubt, my happy Jamaican experience.

By my second term of teaching I realized that something was wrong, however. Yes, I was teaching in a country in which I had not lived before, but this was not a new experience for me. The age groups were the same, the subjects were the same, and so what was the problem? There was no enthusiasm on my part in approaching the job, no sense of accomplishment at the end of a day's teaching, no feeling of empathy with the students. The students. Could that be it? I decided to quietly observe the other teachers and their inter-action with the pupils. It was the result of this investigation which would help me understand what was happening and to conclude that I could no longer remain within that particular profession.

It would appear that in the four-year period in which I had been away both from the region and the experience of interacting with and teaching adolescents, the latter had undergone a change which had transformed them into creatures quite different from what I had known. Third form students, in a school with a fine reputa-tion culturally and academically, located within a country known in the region for its conservatism, had assumed attitudes towards institutions and symbols like schools and teachers with manifested displays of equality bordering on haughtiness instead of the tradi-tional respect. No doubt in so doing they had been influenced by the introduction and spread of cable television throughout the region. Their parents themselves would have been spawned by the new age and therefore exhibited more liberal and conciliatory parenting attitudes.

There had been no opportunity for me to prepare for this change. Not merely had I been away from the region, but neither had there been any occasion in the interim to interface and communicate with adolescents who now presented themselves to me as perfect strangers. The other teachers, in circumstances totally dissimilar to mine, were acting as if it were the norm for students to conduct themselves as if they were on par with their teachers. I knew I had to leave the profession.

There are times when I do wonder if my real reason for reacting in this fashion was born out of that deep-seated vocation to locate myself, not within the walls of a school, but rather within an insti-tution which would give me the opportunity to begin to put into practice the discernment which had been awakened in me during my last years in Geneva. The Caribbean Conference of Churches, an affiliate of the World Council of Churches and one with a programme reflective of that of CCPD, was beckoning me. The programme of Christian Action for Development in the Caribbean (CADEC), the development arm of the CCC, was therefore where I turned my attention in 1977 and my application was successful.

Preparing to Fly!

My sojourn at CADEC took my CCPD experience several steps further along for, having been introduced to and schooled in the theory of development of and for the people – grassroots development – I was ready, almost, to leap into the praxis of said development, with a strictly Caribbean flavour. My entry into the field was gentle, however. I was fortunate enough to be attached to the department which considered for funding projects from throughout the region, usually of an economic nature – from Cuba in the north to Guyana and Suriname in the south. My initial role was administrative, but nonetheless gave me the opportunity to apply to the analysis and development of these projects an approach to development programming with which I had become familiar in Geneva.

Projects could be national, sub-regional or regional in nature and this made more intriguing the challenge to get it right or as close to right as possible. A rather complex administrative system prevailed. I was assistant to the coordinator of the department responsible for these projects, who was located in Barbados with responsibility for giving oversight to project officers located in Jamaica, Antigua, Barbados itself, Trinidad and Tobago and Guyana. The Jamaica project officer was responsible not merely for the projects emanating out of Jamaica but for the entire northern Caribbean. The Antigua-based officer similarly oversaw projects from the Leeward Islands in their entirety, as did the Barbados-based officer for the Windward Islands (exclusive of Grenada) as well as Barbados. Trinidad and Tobago had Grenada, Curaçao and Aruba included within their portfolio and Guyana had additional responsibility for Suriname.

The Projects Development Programme (PDP) was thus, as one might imagine, a gigantic project, certainly the largest within the ambit of the Caribbean Conference of Churches and often the most controversial. Church related politics sometimes played a role as well since the project officers were expected to liaise with the relevant national Councils of Churches, many of which comprised highly conservative but powerful figures within both church and

At a planning meeting in Curaçao

community. The other challenge in this regard was the fact that the composition of these church councils did not always make for a like-mindedness or similarity of views, approaches or even politics! It was an exciting time and, as had happened in Geneva, I was privileged to be part of what was the most challenging and controversial programme within the organization.

Twice yearly there were meetings of the staff of the PDP. These were very important meetings which would consider not only matters of programming but often of policy. While the PDP was powerful and had the largest budget within the organization, it was not nor was it allowed to be a law unto itself. These periodic regional staff meetings would therefore make some broad brush stroke decisions relative to the projects which appeared to be emerging within the region, and where there were sub-regional or regional projects, input would have to be given by all concerned. Sometimes projects of a clearly pioneering nature would emerge, such as one on the harnessing of solar energy which came out of Barbados and went on to become a large and very successful company in its own right. Other times there would emerge projects which had been tried in other places and from which lessons could be learned and applied. The point was that a unified, practical and responsive approach to the development of the programme and the projects within its jurisdiction was where the focus was placed.

The CCC Project Development Programme meets in Havana, Cuba, 1979
with an OXFAM representative among the delegation

As a means of the project staff acquainting itself with the region as a whole, it was the practice to hold these meetings in various parts of the region, with at least one day being devoted to field trips. Meeting the stakeholders and having them meet those who had participated in the development and funding of their projects made for experiences which were, in a word, invaluable. Face to face meetings, where one could relate both successes and problems being encountered, where some advice could be shared or, if not, researched for later sharing with the project holder, often proved to be the highpoint of these meetings. A third approach used was the insertion of a workshop with a particular theme which, for example, could be reflective of some new approach in development programming which project officers might find useful in the undertaking of their work programmes. Hence it was that in 1979 I was presented the opportunity to make my first visit to Cuba – beautiful, old-world Cuba with its vintage hotels and antique vehicles.

The project officers themselves were expected to make periodic visits to their projects both in and out of the locations where they resided. Often on these field trips they would meet with prospective

Some time off from our meeting in Cuba

project holders who had written asking for consideration of their projects and the opportunity would be taken to interview them, delve more deeply into the preparation and execution of the project and, where appropriate, make field visits. All these preparations culminated in a twice-yearly meeting of a powerful regional committee called the Development Fund Committee (DFC).

The members of the DFC were drawn from throughout the region and represented both clerical (of the clergy) and secular persons, some with great professional and academic expertise in their particular field. Because of the way the process had developed, it was not the project officers but the coordinator of the PDP and his staff who were expected to present and defend these projects before this powerful committee. In the entire three years which I spent with PDP, I can genuinely say that the nail-biting anxiety never diminished.

I would say that the most valuable lesson learned in the course of my attachment to this organization was that in the planning and implementation of programmes of a developmental nature and assisting projects in this regard, emphasis must be placed on the structure and administration of the planned activity, key components of which would be communication, team-building, and the inbuilt mechanisms for continuous analysis and evaluation.

The CCC also published a monthly regional newspaper. *Caribbean Contact*, as it was called, was the only such paper to be published anywhere in the region at the time. Liturgical issues were outlined, debated and discussed, as one might expect, it being an organ of the churches. In fact, one of the big liturgical themes was the decolonizing of Caribbean theology. But *Caribbean Contact* also covered regional political and socio-economic topics and events not only as straight reporting but also with an analytical approach, often in fairly controversial fashion. Furthermore, it was a channel for providing information and coverage on the programmes of the CCC.

But how was all this funded? Like the World Conference of Churches, the CCC enjoyed the support of a consortium of funding institutions from Europe, the United Kingdom and North America in the main. Many of these institutions had programme preferences to which their funding would be put. The funding of projects of an economic nature were clear favourites and, once reporting reflected acceptable programming procedures and an account of monies spent, there was usually no problem with the provision of support. There was more to the continuity of funding, however. Periodically, the funding institution would send a representative to the region to engage in discussions with staff persons within the high echelons of the institution as well as to visit some of the projects for a first-hand view of what was happening on the ground. Finally, there were periodic evaluations.

The very word "evaluations" struck fear in some of us within the organization. The evaluators would ultimately be chosen by the funding organization with possibly some input from the recipient organization. A set of terms of reference would be drawn up and the evaluators, usually a minimum of two but sometimes more, depending on the scope of the programme or institution, would have the task of assessing the programme, the operations and finances of the organization, and determine whether they did what they set out to do and if not, why not. In an organization as large as the Caribbean Conference of Churches, the assignment could spread over several weeks and by the time the follow-up period in respect of additional material, reactions and visits was finalized, it could be several months.

This, then, is the context in which I found myself. Not only was the work challenging, but there was the impression that something useful was being done for people who, in the main, could turn to no other financial institution for the funds required to fulfill the goals they had set themselves. There were times when it was not about financial assistance at all, but technical support, of information, of advocacy – the need to have the information put out there. And there were times when it was determined that what was required was an exchange visit, perhaps to another country with a similar context to observe first-hand how the same thing was being done by persons with experience and/or expertise in the field.

After about two years of work in the position of administrative assistant, I was promoted to the position of project officer, a position which now put me in direct contact with project holders and necessitated my travel to other islands in the region, particularly the Windward Islands.

I remember the first time I landed in Dominica. It was 1979, and Hurricane David had earlier struck the Windward Islands. I knew a hurricane had struck but I could not have imagined the devastation I was about to encounter, perhaps because I had never before witnessed the wrath of a hurricane. The plane landed at the Melville Hall Airport and I was momentarily confused at the number of tall trunks I saw standing around the airstrip, until I recognized them for what they really were: decapitated coconut trees. Hundreds of them just positioned there like empty flagpoles. Then into my line of sight came the banana trees, all lying flat on the ground. It was only when the flight attendant touched me on the shoulder that I realized that while all the other passengers had deplaned I was still sitting there in a state of shock and sadness for a people whose livelihoods I knew depended on these two commodities. And that sense prevailed throughout my journey from Melville Hall to Roseau because all along the way stood similar signs of devastation.

Experiences such as these only hardened my resolve to continue in the field of development programming and to do my part alongside and in tandem with organizations which sought to find ways and means of providing responses to those who could not expect to receive support from the traditional established institutions. Little did I guess that both challenge and opportunity to make good this resolve were just around the corner.

Two overseas vacations were taken while I lived in Barbados – one to Jamaica and the other to Haiti. Jamaica, that Fair Isle where once we were so happy, had undergone economic and social changes which rendered it almost unrecognizable. There had occurred a flight of capital and veritable abandonment of the economy by the private sector as a result of the fiscal measures which the government of Michael Manley had put in place. The effects of the oil crisis on the overall economy did not help matters either. Jamaica, unlike Trinidad and Tobago, is not an oil producer and had had to import oil at much higher prices than originally. Assistance had been requested from the International Monetary Fund and the conditionalities which came with their soft loans and grants were harsh. It wasn't long before there were stickers posted throughout the capital, in particular, with slogans that read: IMF? THERE'S GOT TO BE A BETTER WAY! Crime, as one might well imagine, was also on the upswing.

The visit to Haiti in August 1978 turned out to be a heartbreaking but eye-opening experience. We were staying at a friend's house and the relative splendour of this accommodation, including a swimming pool on the grounds, in the context of the widespread surrounding poverty did not make for a happy time. Coming out of a bank one morning where we had gone to change some money, we encountered a group of beggars to whom Frank made the mistake of handing some money. Like a flash, from across the road, oblivious of the traffic going in opposite directions, an old woman dashed towards us with hands outstretched seeking her share. The contrast later came when we visited the craft market where such beautiful paintings, sculptures and the like could be found. It made me wonder at the irony that juxtaposed such exceeding wealth of talent with such poverty of financial resources.

The highlight of the trip came one evening when we visited a voodoo ceremony for which our host used his contacts to gain us entry. The ceremony that evening was dedicated to the god Damballah, one of the most important of all the loa (spirits). Damballah is "the Sky Father and the primordial creator of all life" and is often depicted as a serpent or is closely associated with snakes. He is said to "rule the mind, intellect and cosmic equilibrium" and so, as the drums began to roll, our host himself a Methodist minister, warned us that we had to be careful lest their mesmerizing effect worked its magic on us. As the houngan (the male priest who leads the ceremony) chanted, we realized that a young man had climbed a tall coconut tree situated in the yard where the outdoor ceremony was being held, without the use of his hands! But not only did he climb up the tree the way a snake would, he also slithered down in similar fashion, his body twirled around the trunk and his tongue flickering out of his mouth like a snake's. I was terrified. Is this really a human being or a snake in human form? Might I be similarly affected? (*And those drums, those hypnotic drums!*) I spent so much energy trying not to have the drums have an impact on me that I am not sure I was much conscious of how the rest of the evening unfolded. When we left, mine was a sense of relief!

On March 13, 1979, the world awakened to the news that Grenada had experienced a bloodless coup in which the New Jewel Movement (NJM) had ousted Sir Eric Gairy, the Prime Minister of Grenada, and set up a People's Revolutionary Government (PRG) to take charge of the governance of the country. It was reported that not a single shot had been fired in the process. The world and the Caribbean region in particular, went into shock. Those of us who were in the PDP felt particularly close to the whole process. Not only did we have representation on the main funding committee by one of the leaders of the revolution, but also a number of projects of long timeframe and high value had been approved for Grenada and were already in the works.

The irony was that, given the principles the PRG claimed to stand for, particularly in the context of what the region knew Gairy had represented, it made perfect sense that the CCC and CADEC, would provide support for Grenada. The Council of Churches in Grenada disagreed, however, and for the duration of the revolutionary process, this body remained resolutely hostile to the revolution and its programmes. Comprising mainly members of the Grenada business and social elite, this conservative body continued to be largely critical of the efforts of the PRG throughout the latter's time in power, refusing to give their blessing to any of the major projects. The PDP was therefore forced to provide continued support without the input of the churches.

PDP's Grenadian colleagues were meanwhile excitedly sharing with us their plans for the new Grenada. One such plan was for land tenure for the landless who comprised one third of the population of an island that is mainly agricultural. Projects for the youth also took centre stage.

Reflection and Decision Making Time

While these events occurred at a professional level, at a personal level my life could not be said to be similarly undergoing a revolutionary process filled with promise for the future. On the home front and throughout successive academic terms, Frank was completely caught up in his work. He had attained the position he had planned for and dreamed of and now threw himself entirely into his teaching. He would lock himself for hours in his study to allow for maximum concentration in the preparation of his lectures, leaving me with the full responsibility of taking care of two small children and the household in the bargain. Mind you, whenever I needed to travel he was always very cooperative, very supportive and never grumbled about taking on these responsibilities but once I returned, the normal pattern immediately resumed.

Retrospectively, I can reaffirm that open communication would have helped here – at least I like to think so. I think that at that stage of my life the assumption was made that the partner must be aware that something was amiss and therefore step up to the plate by asking a question or two. Not really. This does not happen in real life. In fact, I have found male partners to be mainly cowards – too timid and afraid to find out what might be going on inside the woman's head, if only to give themselves the excuse of doing nothing about what might be a very serious problem. Despite the many non-verbal ways by which I telegraphed to Frank that something was amiss, that my personal life was far less than perfect, that I needed him to play a more participatory role in the affairs of the family, he either did not hear those silent screams or just decided to shut them out.

Adeline, at my request and because I disliked the idea of her living alone, had come to live with us in Barbados as had happened in Jamaica after my son was born and, to his credit, Frank had raised no objection to the suggestion. Adeline, at 75, still the consummate seeker after academic pursuit and fulfillment, began to nag me about doing a second degree. "Frank has three, what about you? It's your turn now." When I wouldn't take the bait, she started to encourage Frank to get me going. Frank responded in his usual detached, mild and unhurried way that he was not preventing Regina from doing further studies, that if Regina wanted to, she could.

Frank, the academic self-starter par excellence could not possibly understand that it was not her mother's encouragement that Regina needed, but his. It was not communication with her on that or other topics in which I wished to engage, but with him. It would have made all the difference in the world if Frank had been the one to encourage me to engage in further studies. It would have demonstrated to me that he thought I had the wherewithal to go further academically. It would have told me that I was important enough to him to be thinking of me in that way. It would have manifested his willingness to share the responsibility of child rearing and development while I studied.

As it turned out, none of that happened. He never raised the issue with me nor I with him. Indeed, it was one of his own academic colleagues who suggested that I do a certificate course in project development at the Barbados Institute of Management and Productivity (BIMAP). I eagerly accepted the suggestion and completed the course successfully with the assistance of the Caribbean Conference of Churches who sponsored me. Not only did I thoroughly enjoy doing the course but also found it to be exceedingly helpful in the requirements of my job as a project officer.

Simultaneous with all this ferment was the slowly simmering notion in my head that perhaps I needed some kind of break. I know there are those who can isolate the bits of their lives that make them happy and convince themselves that as a result they are contented with life. For me, all the pieces must interlock and I am always prepared to work hard at helping this to happen. But this is not always possible and when effort is neither mutual nor sustained, particularly in the context of non-communication, the process collapses – for me, at any rate. I had to find a way to get on with my life, and neither the society in which I felt so little at home nor the partnership in which I felt no longer fulfilled was providing the answer.

Only my children and my job made me happy and I remember actually planning a move back to Trinidad with them. I had sent my resume to a friend to have her help me find a suitable job – not in teaching but in the field of development programming. In the midst of these events came the request from the Grenada colleagues that I help them realize their plan for the new Grenada. The offer came like a godsend and was accepted with great enthusiasm, despite the challenges which lay ahead at both the personal and the professional levels.

Caribbean Politics in the Context of the 1970s

The seventies, in retrospect, perhaps represented a period when parts of the region had begun to experience self-radicalization, as non-capitalist approaches began to be examined by some of its politicians and non-alignment became a rallying cry in some Caribbean capitals. From as early as 1969, Forbes Burnham, President of Guyana, had established his country as the Cooperative Socialist Republic of Guyana. Then in 1973, there was collective recognition by the four CARICOM countries that existed – Jamaica, Trinidad and Tobago, Guyana and Barbados – of the communist state of Cuba. This was followed up, in 1975, by the majority vote of the Organization of American States (OAS) that the sanctions imposed against Cuba be lifted.

In 1975 too, Michael Manley began to speak of building democratic socialism in Jamaica and of moving the country forward "in the upright" position as opposed to "on bended knee". Meanwhile, Cuba was actively pursuing its overseas support for African independence movements, dispatching thousands of troops to Angola, for instance. Later, Ethiopia during the period 1977–1978 also became the recipient of some 17,000 Cuban troops to assist it in warding off Somali aggression against its territory in the Ogaden region. There was therefore a growing radicalization throughout the Caribbean and by 1979 Grenada and Nicaragua had both joined this group of radicalized governments via their respective revolutions in March and July. During the course of the PRG administration in Grenada, the region was to witness the gaining of considerable support for left-wing parties in the other three Windward Islands – St. Vincent, St. Lucia and Dominica.

Now it seemed it was my time to fly – to create and fill for myself the space which was opening up in my mind and, it seemed, my destiny. Grenada, without any planning of the sort on my part, had now presented itself as the perfect way forward for me, to use the ideas of Geneva and the experiences of CADEC to take my social and intellectual (if not academic) development several steps further. I had no idea what I was stepping into, but my gut instinct told me that I simply had to do it. And, while the experiment ended disappointingly for the PRG and the people of Grenada, in retrospect I know I would not have missed it for the world.

In Grenada, I truly learned to fly. It was a time of beginning for me, for reinventing myself with innovative ability, reframed goals and intentions. A new vision was being launched. For its part, Grenada demonstrated to the region what was and still is possible to achieve when governments and communities work hand in hand for the good of the nation. More than three decades after the collapse of the revolution some of those programmes, at both the government and non-governmental levels, continue to exist and to perform.

Life with Frank had presented me with opportunities – opportunities which very likely I never would have enjoyed had I not married this man who knew where he wanted to go and was determined to take his family along for the ride. He had taught me a great deal as well – to think analytically about world affairs, politics, and religion. He was not a practical person. He could not care less about matters such as paying bills and shopping for food. Nor was he of much help in the child-rearing department, although always willing to do as asked or told. The problem was that I hated having to do either the telling or the asking. "What have I done wrong now?" became a familiar refrain when my heavy silence became too much for him to ignore. Yet, to be able to write this memoir, drawn from such a rich palette of memories and experiences which are not reflected in most people's lives, is entirely due to my life and liaison with Frank and the world which had unwittingly opened up to me via the fulfillment of the dreams which he had for himself.

And it is not just about the past as the past since my present and my future are also based on and firmly linked to this past. The entrepreneur I have become today emerged out of the myriad strands of these experiences, beginning with Jamaica. If I consider myself successful at this point, it is because of the formation of self, of the incremental impact which the multitude of experiences have had on me. This is something which I would urge women to reflect on – the notion of self and what it means to each individual woman – and having reflected, to make a forward move towards implementation. This is rarely an easy move, rarely a decision which comes without challenges but then, how else would one grow?

The Barbados parting of ways was not exactly an amicable one. Frank was upset at my decision and at the time I was angry at the fact that over time he had pushed me into a position where I felt I had no choice but to move on. But, no doubt, because of the children, to whom we were both committed, the relationship continued, contentious and hostile in the beginning, but eventually warming to a level where we are today as comfortable with each other as we were at our initial acquaintance.

It was, however, interesting to note how our friends responded. Human beings are what we are and I suppose it should have been expected that people would take sides. The men were clearly flabbergasted that Regina should take so bold a step as to leave her husband, a husband, moreover who had not shown himself to be either unkind or unfaithful. What more could a woman want, for heaven's sake? In fact, Frank's own mantra, whenever I tried to discuss issues which I felt were of importance to the relationship, was, "But what more do you want? I don't run around with other women and I have never lifted a finger against you...." All true and this, I suppose, was proof of my good fortune and clear evidence that I should toe the line and remain in the relationship. As for some of the wives, the conservative ones who believed that societal norms should always be followed, that a marriage was to be for all time and that if anyone rocked the boat it should not be the woman – well, those women went so far as to stop speaking to me.

This was 1979, after all, and the global village fully united by cable television and the Internet was some distance away. Traditional approaches prevailed. I was Adeline's daughter, however. I had not been raised in a household without the benefit of male support, headed by a woman whom I would come to think of as the "original feminist", to think now that I could not make it on my own. I could and I would. But I remember the reaction of two female friends, both in stable relationships yet open-minded enough to understand my position. Both Joan and Joyce were supportive and Joan went so far as to lend me a book called *Your Erroneous Zones* by Wayne Dyer which I found to be so helpful that over the years I have suggested to several women that they read it. It is a book which helps you to identify yourself and the issues that matter to you, sometimes subconsciously, so that you can pull them out, look them squarely in the eye, and deal with them effectively.

I was on the move, again – this time on my own....

6 ✤ Grenada and My Experience of the Grenada Revolution 1980-1984

ACCORDING TO HISTORICAL accounts, Grenada, though "discovered" by Columbus in 1498, remained uncolonized for over one hundred years, partly because of the presence of the fierce Carib Indians who were the inhabitants of the island at the time and were seemingly prepared to defend it at any cost. In 1650 the French purchased Grenada from the British, brought in additional reinforcements and began to wage consistent battles with the Caribs. Sauteurs (French for "leapers") in the parish of St. Patrick was the final stronghold of the Caribs and it was from a cliff in Sauteurs, now known as Leapers Hill, that (in 1653) the remaining Caribs leapt to their deaths rather than be conquered by the colonists.

Grenada became British in 1763 whereupon hundreds of Englishmen and Scots descended upon the island lured by the prospects of profit in the silver age of plantation development. And plantations did flourish in Grenada – but only for a short while. Much earlier than many of her neighbours, Grenada experienced the collapse of the sugar industry and as early as the mid-nineteenth century, sugar production was virtually abandoned in favour of cocoa, nutmeg and other spices. These crops encouraged the development of smaller land holdings and the rise of a yeoman farmer class. Grenada, like most of her Caribbean neighbours, had, since the early twentieth century, been undergoing growing social inequality, colonial neglect and deterioration of the economy such as it was. Her people yearned for deliverance.

Tiny though it is, Grenada presented a microscopic picture of Third World underdevelopment and misfortune. Take for example, a bar of chocolate which costs well over a United States dollar in many of the developed countries in which it is produced. But how had this come about? First, the cocoa is obtained from a Grenada, or a Ghana, for example, and the sugar from, say, the Caribbean, the locus classicus of the sugar plantation. They then add a little milk obtained from their cows to the sugar and cocoa and thus a chocolate bar is made and presented to the world as a product of that particular country. For the cocoa input the poor peasant receives a few cents and for the sugar input the plantation, too, receives just a pittance. The producing country benefits from the lion's share – the value added – for their ingenuity and industriousness. The plight of Grenada thus epitomizes the anguish of underdevelopment in the Third World.

To be fair, Grenada, since the turn of the twentieth century, had begun to utilize some of its cocoa to produce its own chocolate, progressing to the production of chocolate bars in the twenty-first century. However, most of its cocoa is still exported to the developed world. In 1958, Grenada, along with its West Indian counterparts became a member of the West Indies Federation. When the Federation, however, collapsed after only four years, the British government tried to form a smaller federation out of its remaining dependencies in the Eastern Caribbean. But this, too, failed to work. The concept of associated statehood was applied in 1967 whereby the remaining British colonies assumed responsibility for their internal affairs. In 1974, full independence was granted to Grenada and Sir Eric Gairy became the country's first Prime Minister.

Prelude to the Grenada Revolution

To understand the rise of Sir Eric and the sway he held over Grenada, it should be understood that with the gradual withdrawal of the British, left standing was a small but dominant class of landowners, merchants and state functionaries who not only controlled large parcels of the best land, but also the commodity boards, public utilities and the private sector interests in general. The masses were effectively marginalized, landless and in desperate need of a courageous and articulate leader to champion those considered to be among the dispossessed.

Between 1951 when universal adult suffrage was first introduced and 1979 when he was finally toppled from power by the New Jewel Movement, Eric Gairy's Grenada United Labour Party (GULP) won five out of the seven general elections. A flamboyant figure who consistently dressed in white, Gairy was as revered by many of Grenada's poor as much as he was disliked by the landed elite. Initially, he favoured the landless and working-class Grenadian and many remembered him as the spokesman who stood up for their cause, magnanimously gave gifts of land to those without, and presented himself as a hero to the crowd. But by 1970 the hero had turned villain. By then, Gairy had changed his persona and to his old incompetence was added an authoritarian, brutal and corrupt image. In many cases he instructed the state to purchase the farms of his landed supporters at higher than market value prices and then distributed these among the landless in small parcels.

Gairy, though, did not entirely dominate the political scene in Grenada throughout the period 1951 to 1974. A second political party the Grenada National Party (GNP) had emerged led by a lawyer and representative of the interests of the economic elite. For two terms between 1957 and 1967 the GNP was given the mandate to govern Grenada's affairs. The GNP was as conservative as the GULP was ostentatious and the real problems of the people remained untouched. In 1974 Gairy declared Grenada an independent state amidst the widespread protests of many of his countrymen.

Post-independence, he consistently embarrassed the country by presenting himself at the United Nations to discuss the issue of flying saucers. Moreover, he was said to institute many of his policies and practices on the basis of dreams which he had. He had a huge cross placed on a mountain top, with the notion that it be seen from throughout the island. In a way, he appeared to have been inspired by Haiti's François Duvalier, many of whose methods he copied, down to his goon squad – the Mongoose Gang – similar to Haiti's Tonton Macoutes.

It was against this background that the New Jewel Movement had emerged. Originally inspired by the Black Power movement and the anti-colonial struggles in Africa, early in its development the leadership sought to emulate the example of the Cuban Revolution and to follow Marxist principles. Among the rank and file of Grenada, there appeared to have been a feeling of trust in the young and academically gifted leadership who had spearheaded its formation back in 1973. No doubt because their interests had been generally unrepresented by both the GULP and the GNP, the people of Grenada showed enthusiastic support for the Maurice Bishop-led insurrection which toppled the US-backed Gairy regime on March 13, 1979 and ushered in a popular, anti-imperialist revolution. One-manism, nepotism, ignorance and defamation of women's rights were now to be misdeeds of the past. After the "revo" as it was colloquially called, the NJM immediately set about establishing a government which, according to them, was to be people-led.

To begin with, the leaders were all well known to the Grenadian population, more so given that they had attempted an electoral coalition (unsuccessfully) with the GNP in 1976 and had served as the opposition party since then. The People's Revolutionary Government (PRG), as they now called themselves, suspended the 1974 Constitution, banned all political parties with the exception of the New Jewel Movement and declared Maurice Bishop Prime Minister of Grenada. In addition, trade union representation was to be encouraged, free medical services introduced, education and adult literacy were to be given high profiles, while measures were taken to benefit small farmers and farm workers.

The Land Reform Programme of the People's Revolutionary Government

In March 1980, one year after the revolution came to power, I arrived in Grenada without my children who, it had been agreed, would be allowed to complete the current academic year in Barbados and join me at the start of the August vacation. A furnished flat had been secured for me in the meantime and I would have a few months in which to acquire adequate unfurnished accommodation. The job description had been prepared and an office and staff persons were in place. Moreover, I would have three consultants to assist in the implementation of my duties. So, what were these duties to be?

Noting the twin problems of joblessness and landlessness among the youth sectors of the society, the PRG had created a programme designed to respond to these two key problems. The National Cooperative Development Agency (NACDA) with its slogan, "Idle Lands for Idle Hands", was instituted with me as the director of the programme. Additionally, because the planned mechanism for the youth to establish themselves was via the formation of cooperatives, I was appointed Registrar of Cooperatives with responsibility not only for those new cooperatives which were to be set up, but also those already existing which were in the main credit unions. It was a huge portfolio and the challenge was even greater.

To their credit, the PRG, recognizing the mammoth nature of the task at hand, had not merely handpicked the best of the former

Cooperatives Division staff to work with me as field officers, but had also hired consultants with very specific briefs and the experience required for creating the planned impact of the programme. Thus, it was that my Sri Lankan consultant, Mr. Peiris, was an international expert in the development and functioning of cooperatives; my agricultural consultant, Garth Southwell, had wide regional experience at both the academic and field levels; and the small business consultant, Bob Gordon, had led a very successful programme of a similar nature in Jamaica and was on loan to the PRG by the government of that country, led by Michael Manley.

We launched the programme via a land reform campaign which was publicized throughout the island. This was followed by a series of public meetings organized by village and with the aim of giving those interested the opportunity to find out more about the programme and to encourage them, particularly the youth, to ponder and possibly accept the ideas presented. It was hoped that this would stimulate them to begin the process of implementation in order to make the planned programme a reality. Persons were expected to form their own groups, on the basis not merely of need but also of interest, of trust and commitment to the process. The programme itself was the beneficiary of a rather large sum of money which would be used to assist the groups via the granting of low interest loans. And, of course, there was the technical assistance which was available, not merely to me as the director of the programme, but to the participating groups as well.

A vehicle and driver had also been provided to me and with the children still in Barbados at the start of my tenure, I was able to attend the land reform community meetings at night and to visit by day those groups who thought they had a good idea for a cooperative project. Many were the times that I traversed Grenada, from Sauteurs in the north to Grand Anse in the south, from La Sagesse in the east to Gouyave in the west. Many too were the nights I returned home at midnight, having had to keep a close eye on my not exactly youthful driver, Bubboy, to ensure that he was not falling asleep at the wheel and taking us unwittingly over one of the precipices of the Grand Etang.

But these were exciting times! There was this sense of awakened energy, of new discovery, of finally experiencing the fully integrated practice of development theory. In Geneva, I had developed an understanding of what it meant; in Barbados I had had the opportunity for praxis at the NGO and community-based level; and now here I was in Grenada working with a government which understood that for true development to succeed, there must be backward and forward linkages formed between and among those who governed and the people in the communities.

One of the realities of Grenada at the time was the large amount of unused and uncultivated land which was owned by persons often no longer resident on the island. The youth who came forward as part of the NACDA programme were therefore encouraged to seek out such parcels in their communities, up to ten acres, and the government would then take such land under state control and sub-lease to these cooperative groups for their farming use. NACDA's role was meant to bring the young and perhaps inexperienced into the ambit of the world of work and of entrepreneurship, while combining this goal with the productive use of land resources.

There was, however, a second aspect to the programme of land reform. As part of the Gairy inheritance, the government now found that there were some 25 large estates under its control. As a parallel to what the youth and cooperatives were expected to do, the government established a company called the Grenada Farms Corporation (GFC). This was intended to manage these farms in order to make them well run, profitable and productive for both the local and the export markets.

The revived state farms now operating as the GFC made a deliberate approach to bring within its ambit estate workers who traditionally had represented an agro-proletarian group at the bottom of the economic ladder. Employing at least 1,000 workers across the 25 state farms within its jurisdiction, the PRG established a minimum wage, pensions and other benefits payable to these workers. In addition, there was established a mobile health care unit funded by the Canadians in which a qualified nurse drove from farm to farm on specified days, interviewing workers, taking their blood pressure and basically advising them on good health care practices. Cases found to be serious would be referred either to a health centre within the given parish or to the general hospital in St. George's.

Yet a third component to this programme was established. Grenada's long history of cash cropping and commodity agriculture had produced a class of private farmers of middle size. In an effort to make technical and credit resources available to this farming class, the Productive Farmers Union (PFU) was established with an emphasis on training, technical support, credit and marketing assistance. The Land Reform Programme is a good example of how the PRG created a successful coalition between governance and infrastructure with the people as the natural beneficiary of the overall approach and expected result.

Infrastructurally, and to complete the forward and backward linkages which the PRG hoped to establish and maintain, the Marketing and National Import Board (MNIB) was founded. Not to be confused with the Commodity Boards which traditionally had marketed the various commodities of nutmeg, cocoa, minor spices and bananas produced by Grenada, the MNIB had the task of encouraging diversification within the agriculture sector by encouraging the production of non-traditional crops for which markets would be sought. In addition to the MNIB, the PRG established an agro-processing plant, Grenada Agro Industries located in Grand Anse and processing juices, nectars, jams and jellies for local and overseas consumption. This plant was one of the decided successes of the PRG and the Grenada revolution.

Other developmental approaches

This PRG approach to development comprised conscious efforts to respond concretely to infrastructural as well as socio-economic problems, thereby spearheading the establishment of a number of state enterprises under its stewardship. The Sandino Construction Plant responded to needs in the areas of road reconstruction and repair, housing and the construction of educational and health facilities, for example. The Grenada Sugar Company, devoted, despite its name, to the exclusive production of rum for export, earned valuable foreign exchange for the country and Grencraft marketed the beautiful items produced by the Grenada National Institute of Handicraft mainly from locally available raw materials including found objects.

The members of the PRG continued to be as visible as they were audible and many were the rallies held and the plans shared with the people of Grenada. It was a bid designed to maintain their cooperation and support for a process which, though on the one hand it had received and continued to receive much support regionally and internationally, on the other it faced tremendous condemnation from within and without the region.

It was a perfect time, I thought, at which to hold the general election, the results of which I was sure would be in their favour and would ease their vilification in the eyes of the region and the world at large. Once or twice I raised it with Jacqueline Creft, my friend and a member of Cabinet with responsibility for the education portfolio, but she always seemed impatient at the suggestion. Consideration of this was clearly not on the table. Whether this dismissal was because it appeared to go against the grain of the system they were implementing or was as a result of the negative history and experience of the election process in that country, I could not be certain. In retrospect, perhaps the best explanation I could come up with was that they were afraid that holding elections would legitimize and identify a concrete opposition with which the United States of America could work to advance its counter-revolutionary agenda.

When on June 19, 1980 there occurred a spectacular bomb blast which injured many and blew the legs off one young girl in attendance at the rally, Frank absolutely refused to let the children come to me in Grenada. When I insisted (although in my mind I knew I could guarantee nothing) he told me that if they came and anything happened to them, their blood would be on my hands. I had to back down. We did, however, agree that if nothing untoward happened over the following year, he would allow them to come to Grenada to live with me. I had already moved into our new space, had secured school places for them, and had hired household help which had to be live-in help to accommodate my long working hours. All was put on hold.

Settling into Grenada had been relatively easy since I knew some of the people who were part of the administration. I also became quickly acquainted with members of the cabinet because I headed a programme which the PRG considered of prime importance and therefore had to give weekly verbal reports to them. They were an admirable group. Clearly very bright and very articulate, one was struck by their youth, the oldest being maybe somewhat older than I was and the youngest in their twenties. Indeed, many programme heads were persons in their early twenties and the Assistant Commissioner of Police was a mere 22! They earned one's respect, however, by speaking with one voice and with a level of articulation and conviction which compelled the listener and participant to work even harder to ensure that goals were met.

There were fun times too and I discovered that there were many others, like me, who had come from different parts of the region to make their contribution to the process. Chief among these were

Cubans, Guyanese, Trinidadians and Jamaicans. With the exception of Cuba, Guyana and the Michael Manley administration of Jamaica, none of the governments of the region had accepted the new regime and while the government of Trinidad and Tobago did not, like the others (exclusive of those mentioned above), openly condemn the Maurice Bishop regime, there was no support for it either. The Cubans were a special case and played key roles.

The roads in Grenada were the worst I had ever encountered. It was virtually impossible to believe that any caring government, especially one which like Sir Eric's enjoyed the support of a rural base, could allow its road system to stagnate so dramatically. It was impossible to dodge the potholes and one finally learned how to gently drive through them, which of course strikingly reduced the speed at which one could travel. The natural as well as the built beauty of Grenada more than made up for these shortcomings, however. Like a tiny version of Jamaica, Grenada's lush, mountainous beauty and gentle, exquisite beaches, especially the three-mile long Grand Anse beach, put me completely at my ease. So gentle indeed was Grand Anse Bay that I actually started to learn to swim there!

There was some sentimental attachment to the island as well. This was where Frank and I had honeymooned. Rather than at the guest house as we had planned because it was all we could afford, we had stayed at the Riviera Hotel – a resort located on the beach at Grand Anse. Karl Hudson-Phillips, now deceased and a former close friend of my brother's, had insisted that a hotel and not a guest house be where our honeymoon should be spent. The thin walls of a guest house, he argued, would only make for embarrassment! And to make good his insistence on our choice of a hotel as against a guest house establishment, he had paid for the honeymoon!

Sadly, however, this resort which had comprised attractive separate beach front units had, just over ten years later (like many others of its ilk) deteriorated to the point of being almost unrecognizable. Indeed, Grenada's hotel stock was so vastly impaired that this was one of the projects assumed by the PRG and as a government it literally invested in the establishment and maintenance of one or two hotels. A director of tourism had also been appointed with the task of developing an industry which had been allowed to flounder and thus lose important foreign exchange for the country. The PRG also saw tourism as a means of supporting the agricultural industry of the country, again through backward and forward linkages.

Anyone even vaguely familiar with Grenada's rickety old Pearls Airport in Grenville would have applauded the PRG for their decision to build a new airport given the obvious role it would play and benefits it would bring to achieving an improved tourism industry. Not only was the existing airport several miles distant from the capital and the extreme south of the island where the vast majority of hotels were located, but also it was outfitted with a runway that was capable of accommodating solely propeller aircraft and daytime landing. Only Leeward Islands Air Transport (LIAT), with its fleet of 48 seat propeller planes, could fly to Grenada. This meant that persons wishing to travel to Grenada from outside of the region needed to fly first to either Barbados or Trinidad and then take a connecting LIAT flight to Grenada, a situation that could not possibly have augured well for the tourist industry.

Imagine arriving in the region, having endured a transatlantic crossing, only to have to overnight in a country other than your final destination because your flight might have arrived too late to secure a connection to an airport which had no night landing facilities. One would then need to head back to the airport the following day to take a plane to Grenada. Having landed there, a further challenge, in the navigation of Grenada's roads, usually to the other end of the island where most of the hotels are located, remained to be endured.

Many of the smaller islands such as Antigua and St. Lucia were already in possession of modern international airports, so why the fuss over Grenada? That the government of Cuba chose to support this initiative by providing a skilled work force for its construction was the cause of much rancour with the United States which stridently opposed it. The notion that Cuba would be gaining a foothold in a part of the region which the United States sought to keep under its wing, so to speak, was anathema to the latter. But it was not merely Cuba that supported the construction of the airport. The European Economic Community (EEC) was also providing assistance.

Sunday afternoon drives were often taken to the new international airport to admire its progress and the hard work going into it. Nor were there any security measures which prevented the public from going into any particular area or areas of the site. It was always with some measure of amusement that we would learn from the Reagan administration via the Barbados and Trinidad and Tobago newspapers that underground bunkers were being built for any number of sinister purposes. When the United States invasion finally came, I waited for news of the discovery of these bunkers but, like the weapons of mass destruction in Iraq, news of this discovery never came.

Clearly as a result of the presence of the large number of Cuban nationals, representing airport workers, teachers within the school system and medical personnel at the hospital and health centres, Cuba had an embassy presence in Grenada. The decidedly romantic turn which my life took halfway through my stay in Grenada emanated from this source.

Uh-oh!

Luis, all of 12 years my junior, was serious-minded, dependable and acceptable to both of my children who never tired of his patient company. This mostly platonic relationship took a serious turn when one afternoon, returning from a parent teacher association meeting with my children who had by then joined me in Grenada, we heard a noise coming from inside the house while I was opening the front door. It was 1983 and I was enjoying my stay in Grenada so much and the children were doing so well that I had bought a house on Old Fort – a beautiful old house with a view that reached right across St. George's and down to the south of the island to Point Salines where the new international airport was being built. The plan was to spend the rest of my life in Grenada and certainly to raise my children there, in a society which understood and implemented what development principles were all about.

We assumed that the noise had been made by our cat which might have been inadvertently locked inside, until my son saw a young man running away from the house. Petrified with fear I found myself unable to enter the house and instead sent my son to a neighbour's home to ask him to escort us inside and ensure that everything was all right. The gentleman, in his late seventies (or so he seemed to me), came immediately, armed with a gun which I did not know he possessed and immediately fired some shots in the air after the perpetrator who had long disappeared. (I was of course too frightened to be even remotely amused by his antics until long afterwards.) He then accompanied us into the house, checked all the rooms and ascertained that no one was still there.

I had just had the house burglar proofed but there was a section comprising only jalousies which had been kept in such pristine state that I thought it a shame to put burglar proofing over it and had thus left it intact. Well, this was precisely the section that our intruder had seen as the weak point and used to smash his way in. My friend Jacqui, then a minister of government, sent two armed members of the government security services over to keep watch – I was, after all, a foreign national and the PRG always took special care of its foreign nationals. Luis, when contacted, came over at once and declared that he was certainly not going to leave us without his protection. And the rest, as they say, is history – a history, however, which neither of us nor, for that matter, most persons in Grenada could ever have imagined.

By this time, I was no longer involved with the NACDA programme. I had earlier begun to experience some pressure in coordinating it, a stress born of the perceived need of the PRG to micro manage its implementation given how important this programme was to them. This I was unwilling to endure and had thus requested a meeting with my line minister to discuss the issue and the possibility of relocating to Trinidad. I shall never forget the morning when I received a phone call from the prime minister that he was sending his driver for me so that we could discuss the situation at hand. The driver duly arrived and took me to the prime minister's residence which also served as the location where central committee and cabinet meetings were held. When I walked into the room, it was the entire cabinet which sat there awaiting me, their task obviously being to talk me out of leaving Grenada, whatever it took.

It was Bernard Coard, a man whose extreme brilliance surpasses even his immense sense of self and ambition, who clinched the deal. Bernard actually remembered that in the course of my meetings with him over the fifteen months or so that I had spent in Grenada, I had made allusions to my experience, ability and indeed passion in the preparation of project proposals for fundraising and working with grassroots organizations. I had made no suggestion to him, had expressed no desire to him to move away from what I was at the time doing – but he remembered, nonetheless. On the basis of this recollection, Bernard Coard sat in that meeting and, clearly thinking on his feet, carved out the outlines of a new organization which I would head and whose aims and objectives were exactly what I had mentioned to him, *en passant*, were my preferences. I was floored, captivated, and sold.

"But what shall I say to my mother?" I countered. "She is expecting me and has put things in place to receive me." The response this time came from Maurice Bishop, not so much the brilliant strategist as the people person that he was. Maurice said to me, "Do you want me to write your mother, explaining to her that we need you here and asking her to allow you to stay?" The offer was eagerly accepted by me since I had no idea what I would or could say to her – and Maurice immediately penned his letter which he then folded, placed in an envelope, sealed, addressed and handed to me. All told, I describe this little cameo of events to demonstrate how the revolution had the genetic combination, the DNA by which to succeed and how, when used skillfully, the various chemistries within the upper echelons of the movement were able to turn a situation to their advantage. Between these two leaders, they had succeeded in their quest to have me stay on in Grenada.

The Agency for Rural Transformation (ART) – as we agreed to name the organization – came into being in August of 1981 with the objective of working with the organizations representing farmers, youth, women, health and education. ART would assist them in programme development and implementation, fundraising, and by engaging in ongoing monitoring and evaluation and reporting to the funding agencies. The literacy programme entitled the Centre for Popular Education and the health programme run for the workers of state farms were new to my portfolio as well and there was the opportunity to become acquainted with the broad spectrum of development programming taking place on the ground in Grenada. I could not have been happier.

Flying High!

Here was the opportunity to broaden my knowledge base of grassroots organizations which operated in Grenada and, utilizing the awareness of the programmes in which they were all engaged, ensure that coordination and networking occurred. Moreover, my regional experience could be brought into play not simply via acquaintance with similar projects which had evolved and were developing in the region, but also on the basis of my familiarity with the organizations which funded projects in the region. In addition to raising funds for these programmes, and in consultation with my Board of Directors (comprising representation from each of these grassroots organizations to ensure transparency), it was agreed that a small percentage of each project approved would be put into a special interest-bearing account with a view to ultimately investing in a project aimed at the self-sustenance of the agency. There were other spin-offs as well.

CUSO International, a Canadian development agency (formerly known as CUSO, Canadian University Services Overseas), had made Grenada its Eastern Caribbean base. It facilitated programme coordination of the agencies which it funded (ART included) by convening twice yearly meetings to discuss the progress of the programmes and to present country profiles. These profiles outlined the current status of the respective economies and presented what the project holders saw as future trends. The meetings broadened the perspectives of all participants and with Grenada in the forefront of development programming in the region (at least as development activists saw it) the experiences from this country were always valuable.

There was also a great deal to learn from other project histories, useful in the Grenadian context. Indeed, it was out of the meetings and shared experiences of these organizations that there emerged the umbrella body, the Caribbean People's Development Agency (CARIPEDA), with membership comprising agencies from Belize in the north to Guyana in the south.

CARIPEDA's role was the coordination of programmes of a regional or sub-regional nature such as those of advocacy, communication, exchanges and the like. It was on the basis of the sharing and inputs into processes such as these that, some years later, I was appointed the Caribbean representative on the Board of Directors of CUSO International. Opportunity to travel outside of the ambit which the CUSO/CARIPEDA linkage provided was also made possible. Cuba and Nicaragua were on the agenda quite early since it was felt that the experiences of these two countries could be of great value to the task I was now performing. The Nicaragua experience, similar in history and almost the same age as that of Grenada, was particularly useful. Their movements of women and of farmers had proven up till then to be very successful and would teach me a great deal by way of approaches and strategies to be applied in my dealings with similar organizations in Grenada.

In 1982 came the opportunity to return to the Soviet Union where discussion of the Soviets as separate countries had already begun. This time it was to visit Tallinn, Estonia as part of an African/ Asian/Caribbean delegation organized by the United Nations. It is the non-programme part of the trip that I remember mostly: having to dodge young men who stood outside of the hotel asking you if you had jeans for sale; committing the cardinal error of asking for Russian dolls in a store where a wide variety of craft items were sold, yes, but in a state which prided itself on the independence for which they were already reaching. Watching the group of clearly hostile Estonians who were made to wait outside of the shop in beastly cold weather while the visitors shopped in comfort and further, being told the story about the churches, it came as no surprise to me to learn that Estonia was among the first to declare itself independent of the Soviet Union, given the indications which I saw from as early as 1982.

By 1983 therefore, life as I lived it was wonderful. Not only did I love my job because I found it to be fulfilling of the needs of the communities I had come to Grenada to serve but the results of my efforts were also positive. Sitting in an office was not my style. It was much more interesting to go out into the field and hear what plans people had for themselves and their communities and assist them to meet these needs. The Productive Farmers Union, for example, needed to establish a building which would also serve as a depot where farmers could buy at a cheaper rate, supplies which would be purchased in bulk by the organization. It would also serve as a collection point for produce to be sold to the Marketing Board. Additionally, there would be facilities for meetings and training which would be provided by the various regional and international agricultural organizations operating in Grenada. The Agency for Rural Transformation was able to present for funding a proposal which was subsequently approved for the construction of this building.

The children had settled down to life in Grenada and were doing well at school. In fact, Frank Ayodele had taken the 11+ Examination and passed for his school of choice. He had even agreed to some extra-curricular activities such as I had been trying to impress on him for some time but without success. He had complained to his father that the boys with whom I sent him to play football were very rough and Frank in turn complained to me. I was only trying to toughen him up for the world out there but maybe that was going too far. I desisted and agreed to wait until he was ready. The children spent their holidays with Frank and I spent Christmases with my mother and although I always noticed changes in their girth when they reappeared in Grenada after spending six weeks with Frank I kept my peace and tried to reverse the damage in the months ahead. Luis, my Cuban partner, continued to get along fabulously with us all. The blow, when it came, was sudden and completely unanticipated.

The Bubble Bursts

I suppose the writing had been on the wall since the beginning of October but I had chosen not to do the reading or to connect the dots. To my simple mind, the members of the PRG had too much riding on their collective efforts and reputation to do anything to jeopardize the process. Why, when they knew that the Reagan administration was poised to pounce at the slightest error made, would they play into their hands so easily? Moreover, we were just months away from celebrating that all-important 5th anniversary of the Revolution – a landmark that many did not expect could be reached! I therefore dismissed, completely out of hand, the rumours that I heard as counter-revolutionary propaganda. What an error on my part!

Reality hit me right between the eyes one morning when the husband of my assistant, Val, whom I was picking up at her home to take to work, pulled me aside and told me in low tones that he had it "on very reliable grounds" that the "comrades" had Maurice under house arrest and were planning to hold him there until he agreed to certain demands that were being made by Coard and his followers. So convincing was I in my rebuttal of this information that I could see that my informant half-believed the correctness (and the logic) of what I was saying. But as I left him and drove to work, nagging doubts began to enter my mind. I dropped Val off at the office and promptly returned home to confront Luis with this information. Surely, he would know. And he did. Having listened to what I had to say, Luis uttered not a word in response but instead turned away from me and began to get dressed for work. That was when I reacted… in extreme fashion.

I ranted against what I now viewed as the flagrant stupidity of a man named Bernard Coard whom up to then I had considered to be one of the most brilliant persons I had ever met. I ranted against his obvious lack of knowledge of the Grenadian people who loved Maurice Bishop and his magnetic charm – a leader who made efforts to reach out to and involve the rank and file of the population in the programmes of the revolution, voluntary and otherwise. The populace was a far cry from loving Coard with a similar intensity.

The aims and methods pursued by Coard and his followers seemed more in keeping with those of the privileged bureaucracy administered by Joseph Stalin and were quite removed from the experiences, aims and aspirations of the Grenadian people. "If Bernard Coard thinks he can get away with this plan, then he must be either stupid or just crazy!", I exclaimed to the silent Luis. "The masses of the Grenadian people would never support him. Has he forgotten about the structures for people's participation which *he* was instrumental in setting up? Structures such as mass organizations and zonal councils? Does he have his nose to the ground?" Well, of course Bernard Coard never asked my opinion and one wonders whom, if anyone, he consulted.

It appeared that Bernard Coard was so totally oblivious to the popular structures designed specifically to curb one-manism that he would not have listened to any words of caution against such seemingly rash decision making. Or maybe, having gone through the motions of establishing them for the purpose of form rather than substance, he deliberately kept these structures as small and as weak as possible, ensuring that true power lay in the hands of his faithful lieutenants of whom there were quite a few.

What could possibly have made Bernard Coard think he would get away with this, US intervention or not? Could it have been overweening ambition or such deep immersion in the politics of Marx that he could not see the wood for the trees? Whatever the reason, what I do know is that Bernard possessed skills of persuasion so powerful that if he so wished, he could lead almost anyone down any garden path of his choice. Almost anyone; but not the Grenadian masses.

Bernard also held the additional advantage of having conducted classes in revolutionary Marxist theory to young persons who had by then been elevated to important ranks within the military, party and administrative hierarchy; persons who would clearly be minded to follow and agree with the arguments which he would be presenting for joint leadership of the party. Indeed, some say that from the very beginning, drawn from this pool of talent he trained, Coard had devised a secret faction loyal to himself. And so, it seemed, the cards became stacked against Maurice Bishop.

On Wednesday, October 19, 1983, six days after Maurice had been placed under house arrest, I awoke and prepared myself and my children for work and school, determined that, if I willed it to happen, this would be a normal day like any other. When I said goodbye to Luis that morning, little did I think it would be the last time. I had heard that there was a plan for a popular uprising by the masses of the people who opposed the palace coup. The country had begun to organize. Led by secondary school students in uniform, some 30,000 people banded together, with the objective of marching to Maurice's temporary prison and setting him free.

At around 10 a.m., I heard the chanting of these young persons below my office window and was not surprised. There they were, hundreds of them in school uniform, peacefully marching along the street and chanting slogans in support of Maurice Bishop and the Revolution. I felt swollen with pride at their courage, their determination, their support of a process which they were obviously convinced was to their advantage. To this day, the recollection of that scene causes my skin to tingle. The plan, apparently, was to march to the residence of Maurice Bishop, where he was being held, confront the members of the People's Revolutionary Army (PRA) who were holding him hostage, and to forcibly, if necessary, free him from his temporary prison and reinstate him as Prime Minister.

It was immediately after the passage of the demonstrating students that the drama began in earnest for me. I looked up and, in the middle of the morning, saw my son silently standing in the office. The principal of the Roman Catholic college he was attending had closed the school and sent home all the students. That was when I knew I could no longer pretend that things were normal.

Closing the office and sending the staff home, I drove like a crazy woman to the school my daughter attended, merely intent on ensuring that my children and I got home and to safety. Going at full speed and rounding one of those blind corners so frequently encountered in St. George's, I came face to face with a faceless piece of equipment which up till then I had seen only on a cinema screen. It was an armoured personnel carrier from which protruded an excessively long gun barrel and inside which it was impossible to see anything. I almost ran off the road in shock and fright at the appearance of something I didn't even know existed in Grenada.

Back home, safe and sound, we settled down to watch, from our verandah, events as they now began to unfold in the middle of St. George's. I was joined by friends who came by to check on me and many were the overseas calls which I fielded from those relatives, friends and funding agency representatives, concerned by what they had gleaned about events on international radio and television. It was therefore with a sense of joy and relief that we finally saw the crowd of schoolchildren, now joined by adult supporters, coming down Lucas Street with Maurice Bishop, hoisted on the shoulders of those in the lead. What a celebration there was in my house! But wait. Where are they going? Why aren't they going to the Market Square where all the rallies are held? Why are they going to Fort Rupert (originally Fort George but renamed after the father of Maurice Bishop who had been killed by Gairy's Mongoose Gang back in 1974)?

The spirit of celebration turned to one of puzzlement on our part when we noticed, in the wake of the celebrants who were climbing the hill to the Fort, two of those fearful looking machines, similar to the one which had almost run into me earlier on. Before we could ask ourselves, what was happening, and before our horrified eyes (since we could witness the whole event from my verandah), these armoured personnel carriers began to shoot directly into the crowd of people who were climbing the fort, singing and dancing with Maurice on their shoulders. Surely this was not happening? Surely, I was dreaming? Surely a group of revolutionary leaders who had proclaimed in word and in deed how much they cared for their people would not engage in such a vile act of terror?

From my verandah, I could hear the screams of the victims and it was Leapers Hill enacted all over again. With no other point of exit (it was after all a fort) and blocked by the artillery firing upon them, I watched as people leaped over the edge of that fort, quite substantial in height, and into the crashing waves and rocks below. Mesmerized, I watched this scene – so happy one minute, so bloody the next – before I realized that my young children too were witnessing it. If this was more than my adult mind could grasp, how could they be handling it? Wordlessly, I sent them inside to wait it out.

By about three o'clock that afternoon, the sole activity we could witness on the Fort was the heavy presence of military vehicles and we could only torture ourselves about what had really happened. Then came an announcement from General Hudson Austin which was aired over and over throughout the rest of the afternoon and into the evening. The announcement indicated that at 10 p.m. that evening there would be an official statement aired, of great importance to all in the country. My friends had decided that we should all hear the announcement together and so we all waited with bated breath. While the children played together (there were five of them) we wondered, worried, speculated but never actually guessed at the gruesome news that would greet us at 10 o'clock that evening.

How could one, in 1983 and residing in one of the most peaceful spots in the world, ever begin to imagine the assassination of the Prime Minister, particularly one as beloved as Maurice Bishop, not by a perceived enemy but by a "comrade"? I will never forget the words contained in the announcement made by General Hudson Austin, leader of the self-styled Revolutionary Military Council (RMC) which had taken over the leadership of the country:

> Comrade sisters and brothers, this afternoon, forces counter to the interests of the people of Grenada attempted to engage in action that could only be declared subversive and the revolutionary forces of the People's Revolutionary Army were forced to respond to this action. In the ensuing exchange, some persons were unfortunately killed. Dead are: Maurice Bishop, Jacqueline Creft, Unison Whiteman...

I had stopped listening. Maurice? Dead? Jackie? Dead? Not possible! But the voice had continued to intone, "With immediate effect, and until further notice, anyone caught on the streets of St. George's and environs will be shot on sight!"

By this time, I had stopped listening altogether and didn't realize I was wailing, along with the other women present, until the children ran out of the bedrooms, alarmed and frightened and started shaking us. I remember that there were no words. I remember that we held onto our children and embraced each other, just sobbing helplessly. When we remembered Jimmy, the only man present and husband of one of the women, we found him on the verandah hurling whatever came to hand with all the force he could muster, down the hill at the side of the house, and shouting expletives at the top of his voice. Even after we had calmed him down and put the children to bed, we sat staring at each other in utter disbelief. There was just too much to process all at once.

They had killed the prime minister of the country and others of their own group and party; they had killed my friend Jacqui, thus leaving her young son an orphan; they had decidedly opened up the gates to those who had always opposed the revolution; they had betrayed their own people totally and destroyed the programmes which we had sought so hard to develop and to implement. Where did we stand in all this? If they could have their own pay the ultimate price, for the sake of power, what would be our position? With the exception of Jimmy, we were all foreign nationals. How was I to protect my children? What would I say to their father? I thought too of those who, I was sure, had died as a result of their leap into the sea below the fort. What had happened to them? What were their families to do? Questions all serious but which no one could answer.

The curfew had taken immediate effect and so everyone had to stay put. Luckily, I had shopped for food the day before and the house was able to accommodate the three families. It was late the next evening when a convoy of vehicles swept into my driveway and Hudson Austin himself emerged from one of them. He had come to speak with Jimmy who was a senior public servant. (We have no idea how they knew where he was to be found.) While he waited for Jimmy to appear, the man actually had the nerve to engage in small talk with the women, each of us combing our respective daughter's hair. Frightened to death and filled with hostility as well, we tried to be polite to him but it was very difficult. When Jimmy finally emerged, he took him aside and spoke in low tones and Jimmy took his leave of us all with a sad and serious face. We had no idea where they were taking him or if we would ever see him again. That is what we were all thinking but no one dared verbalize it until his eventual return close to midnight. Naturally none of the women turned in until he came back.

The meeting, as it turned out, was an obligatory assemblage of all the permanent secretaries of the various government ministries to update them on events and to engage in forward planning under what would now be a new administration led by the Revolutionary Military Council. It was a plan that would never materialize.

On the Saturday following the assassination of Maurice Bishop, the RMC announced that they were lifting the curfew temporarily to allow people to get back to their homes, to acquire food, etc. It would however, be reimposed later in the day and would run from sundown to sunup until further notice. My friends all returned to their respective homes and I was left to my own devices with children whose questions I could not answer. Imagine having to confess to my son that I was not sure when he would be seeing his father again. And then, in what I believe to have been a deliberate move by the RMC, because of the many international calls I was receiving and what I had been saying to these callers, my telephone connection was unceremoniously cut.

What a sad period that was for me! In less than two weeks I had gone from euphoria to melancholy, from hope and expectation for the future to despair and gloom. I had already decided that I could no longer reside in Grenada – everything had changed. But apart from this decision I had no idea nor could I do any more than reflect on the present, so volatile and so dangerous. Fortunately for me I had two single male neighbours who occupied apartments on the other side of the street where I lived. Carol, the Jamaican and Alix, the Haitian took turns "babysitting" me and the children in a context in which I, as a mother, was unsure of how to protect her children and we all, as foreign nationals, felt afraid and insecure.

On Monday October 24, the Trinidad and Tobago Government announced that it had taken a decision to send one of its aircraft to Grenada on the following day to collect those of its nationals who wished to return home. I almost fainted with relief and immediately set about packing essentials for me and my children to take with us. I knew that I would be returning – I had to – but it was important to remove the children from this context of insecurity. Frank still lived in Barbados and I would find a way to get them over to him. With my phone cut and the curfew in force, all I could do was send a message to him via a proxy that we were all right but I know that he longed to communicate with his children. The news of the plane to Trinidad came just before the curfew was to be reimposed and I remember taking courage into my hands and stealing away to my office to write a note to the staff and leave them salary cheques since I was not sure how long I would be away. All was set for departure – clothes and other essentials packed and luggage stored in the vehicle, staff taken care of, arrangements made for my Jamaican and Haitian neighbours to keep an eye on the house.

Who Could Have Imagined?

On Tuesday morning, the unthinkable happened. At about 5.30 a.m. my son came into my room and shook me awake saying, "Mummy, I think the Americans are landing." Bleary-eyed and disbelieving, I followed him onto the verandah from which a clear view of Point Salines was possible and for the second time in about six days witnessed a sight that up to that point I had viewed only on a big screen. This time it was a fleet of helicopters from which soldiers were landing via parachutes. One after the other they came without a break, and from each one I counted 50 soldiers. I also counted 50 helicopters and since the military action had begun before I started counting I knew there were more than 50. I turned on Radio Free Grenada to hear what the local authorities were saying and there was the announcer, clearly cognizant of the fact that the Americans had landed on Grenadian soil, and doing her best to whip up a spirit of defiance and courage among her listeners.

Suddenly, at 6 a.m. the radio lapsed into silence, but not for long. There now emerged a strong, male, American voice announcing that the United States forces had landed in Grenada on a "rescue" mission and that control of the air and seaports had been assumed. "Any aircraft," he intoned, "spotted within 50 miles of Grenada airspace will be shot down." My hopes of returning to Trinidad that day were now effectively dashed. BWIA would no longer be coming to my rescue. Operation Urgent Fury, as the Americans called their "rescue mission", was underway. Who could ever have guessed that the United States' determination to enter Grenada would actually have been facilitated, and easily so, by Grenadian revolutionaries – bloody executioners of a crime against their own, a crime too numbing and too shattering to allow for any kind of meaningful response within the region by those opposed to it?

I slumped into so dispirited a mood at this course of events that any maternal sense of responsibility was almost entirely abandoned. When my son assumed a foetal position which I knew to be indicative of something negative, I just watched, powerless to intervene. When he gave up his normal creative endeavours of story writing and architectural drawing of cities, I didn't have the energy or the motivation to encourage him to return to them. It was my daughter, not even eight years old at the time, who rose to the occasion. She repaired to the kitchen and prepared little sandwiches for everyone and brought them out on a tray with drinks and generally retained her cheerful and talkative demeanour which kept us all going.

The American forces had entered Grenada accompanied by soldiers from Jamaica (then under the leadership of Edward Seaga who had assumed power after the October 1980 election). Barbados and the OECS also participated but, interestingly, the Trinidad and Tobago government then led by Mr. George Chambers opted not to. Guyana, the Bahamas and Belize – none of these states took part in the exercise. Nor did any Latin American country. Prime Minister Margaret Thatcher of the United Kingdom is reported to have urged

President Reagan the day prior to the invasion to prevent any action to remove the Marxist government, indicating that she found the prospect "deeply disturbing". The *TNT Mirror* dated November 14, 2014, published the full transcript of the telephone conversation between Prime Minister Thatcher and President Ronald Reagan released by the Margaret Thatcher Foundation. It seemed obvious that not only was she was unsupportive of the intervention but was in fact furious that the action had been taken without either consultation or her agreement. A comfortable political relationship between these two heads of state had, however, been built over time and Harrier jets and pilots were thus supplied. There were no reports of the presence of British troops on the ground.

The bombing began later that same day and it seemed that they were dropping literally all around us. The fact is that St. George's boasts three forts: Fort George, Old Fort and Fort Frederick. I am not clear about the reason for bombing Fort George – since the RMC military action had already taken place there and was over and done with. It was, however, sad for me to witness the total destruction by a Harrier jet of the wonderfully preserved cannon standing resplendent on the Fort. The Harrier jet – an awesome and elegant machine – was as precise in its aim. From my living room and verandah, I watched as target after target was screamingly destroyed on Fort George before this deadly machine turned its attention to Fort Frederick.

There must have been intelligence communicated to the invading forces that the members of the RMC were bivouacked at Fort Frederick but it seems that their precise location had not been ascertained since the first set of bombs which fell on Fort Frederick were aimed at the Richmond Hill Mental Hospital also located there. According to subsequent reports, over 30 mental patients were killed in that assault.

The problem for me was that Old Fort where I lived was located *between* these two forts and I could only guess that our turn might be next. Frantic with fear, I made my children lie beneath my bed for hours while I stood guard – not that I could stop anything but at least I would see it coming. Then at night there were the flares. I don't know about the Cubans but I can tell you that the Grenadian forces did not give up without a fight and I witnessed at least two helicopters struck down by these soldiers and collapsing in fiery heaps.

And what of the torment of a mother, finding herself and her children in a life-threatening situation by no means of her creation but totally unable to protect them? No one (except those who have experienced events of a similar nature) can even begin to understand the trauma. When I stood guard at the entrance to my home while my two poor innocents lay obediently below my bed, I knew that I, indeed all of us, could be struck down at any moment. The difference was that I would see it coming but my children might somehow be shielded from the sure knowledge that they would be killed. By a bomb dropped from a Harrier jet, by a bullet from the gun of any one of the assailants... it didn't matter... to my mind, American, Caribbean or Grenadian military were now, each and every one, the enemy.

The impact of war and conflict as experienced by the people on the ground who had had no part either in the reasons for the conflict or in the decision to take action of any kind can only be imagined by those who have not had to endure it. And while one might argue that there was good reason generally for the decisions taken by the hierarchical structures for such engagement, the fact remains that the cost of such conflict to the innocents can sometimes never be erased nor wounds ever healed. Despite my best efforts, my son was never the same after Grenada.

By Friday, October 28th I had had enough. I had been frightened for long enough and my rights had been trampled on for too substantial a time. There had to be a way to get out of Grenada with my children. Leaving them in the care of my Jamaican neighbour, I boldly drove onto the Main Street and accosted the first American soldier I encountered. Not waiting for him to address me I said, "I am a foreign national living in Grenada and would like to leave. Where can someone give me information?" Not responding in a similarly belligerent fashion to how I had addressed him, he said, "You must go down to Queen's Park, ma'am, and someone there will tell you what to do." Going immediately to Queen's Park, I was directed to a tent in which sat a soldier who appeared anxious to help. He advised me to return the following day with my children and our passports because they planned to leave as soon as they had a full military helicopter load. They would be landing in Barbados, however, he said since they had had no agreement with the Trinidad and Tobago Government. This was even better news for me since I would then be able to hand the children directly over to Frank who for all this time since the invasion had not heard from us. Could one begin to imagine the emotional pain he had to have been experiencing? Where were his children? Were they safe? Unharmed? Would he have the opportunity to see them? Chat with them? The world knew that there were casualties, but who? How many? How? With no local or international media on the ground, all the outside world could do was guess.

But I felt I could not leave without at least ensuring that Luis was all right, never mind I could not communicate with him. I asked the Haitian neighbour to accompany me on an outing that would take me past the Cuban Embassy. I had to at least make the effort to see him before I left. The Cuban Embassy was located on a hilly residential enclave called Morne Jaloux and when I arrived there, what appeared to be hundreds of American soldiers, armed to the teeth with heavy duty weapons and grenades, were strung out in groups of several score each from the foot of the hill right up to the entrance to the embassy on both sides. And the tension on their part was clearly nail-biting.

Moving past the embassy at the slowest pace that I could, I ventured to feign ignorance and ask one of the young soldiers what was happening there. "It's the residence of the Cuban Ambassador, ma'am, and he has diplomatic immunity so we can't enter." Well, they surely had done the next best thing! I was stopped at least three times, asked to step out of the vehicle while they searched the trunk and interior. Call it timing, if you will, but as we crawled past, the door of the embassy suddenly opened and out strode the Ambassador himself with Luis, among others, in tow. Urged forward by the young soldier, I nevertheless came to a full halt and our eyes met sadly in wordless greeting. It was with a bittersweet sentiment that I left the embassy environs. I was happy to know that he was alive and that we had seen each other but ignorance of what fate held in store for him made me sad.

It was only some time later, much later, when rational thinking and the ability to connect the dots came into play on my part once again, that I realized that the little scenario I had witnessed was the surrender by the Cuban Ambassador and his people to the American troops who surrounded them. To his credit, Ambassador Rizo walked tall and strong and with an expression of complete hauteur and resolve in his facial expression and manner generally, as did the personnel surrounding him, Luis being one of them, right up in front where I could see him as plain as day. What a coincidence of timing! That vision has never left my mind. I suppose it's anybody's guess what happened to them once they were taken into custody. Were they interrogated? If so, how? Were they treated humanely? How were the arrangements for their return to Cuba organized, given the enmity and lack of accord between the two countries? Which intermediary country played a role in this regard? What awaited them on their return to Cuba? Were they blamed for not taking the opportunity to offset the potential and later, actual crisis between the warring factions within the People's Revolutionary Government?

The Americans claimed that theirs was a rescue mission invading Grenada since there were about 1,000 Americans living on the island including some 600 students resident at the St. George's Medical School in Grand Anse. Mindful of what had occurred in Iran in 1979 with the fall of the Shah, the Americans were obviously bent on seeing that a similar hostage taking did not occur in Grenada. But the RMC had no such plan on their agenda and the security of the students was never in jeopardy.

I had passed on to Merle Hodge, another Trinidadian who lived in Grenada with her son, the news that we were to be transported out of Grenada the following day, Saturday, October 29. I left the house in the care of Carol, my Jamaican neighbour, who took us to our point of departure. Merle and her son and I along with my children were transported out of Grenada that day in an aircraft which boasted the most rudimentary of facilities. It was either a military helicopter or a cargo plane – I don't recall. What I do recall is the scene that met us on arrival in Barbados.

We arrived unannounced, but scores of media personnel who had been denied entry into Grenada were waiting at the airport, all wanting to interview those of us who had had the experience. Naturally, I declined. My first responsibility was to let Frank know we had arrived by taking his children to him. I tried to take a taxi and the first question which the insensitive driver asked was what currency I had. He refused to take me when he heard I had Eastern Caribbean dollars. Most of the Barbadians standing around cried shame on him but he was undeterred. In the end, I had no choice but to call a friend who lived close to the airport to fetch us and take us to St. Michael where both Frank and my sister Marina resided.

I will never forget the facial expression and body language displayed by Frank when he opened his front door to see his children running towards him. In some sad, pointless way I felt that I had let them all down and not kept the promise of laughter and happiness which we had begun to share and experience in Grenada. But there was nothing to do but soldier on in the face of the reality that my dreams and my expectations had been totally destroyed by a group of people who, less than five years earlier, had held aloft a promise and a vision of democracy and caring to which I had been introduced by my colleagues in Switzerland.

Contact was made with my funding agencies in the United Kingdom and in Holland and I was asked to visit for purposes of debriefing – they also needed to decide what they were going to do about their projects in Grenada particularly in light of the fact that I was no longer going to be there but would be returning to Trinidad. They all agreed that they would ask to have their funds repatriated and the agency which financed the administrative expenses of ART took a decision that each staff person should be given a total of six months' salary to tide us over while we sought new employment. It did not occur to me that the Agency for Rural Transformation would be the single NGO project that the Interim Advisory Council (the new administration which now ran Grenada's public sector affairs) would decide should continue its operations.

My return to Grenada took place about a month later, in a state of some trepidation. I had heard while in Europe that certain names had been placed on blacklists, based on information supplied by certain members of the public. Blacklisted persons were being interrogated intensely at the airport and in some cases were not being allowed entry to the country. Such was not to be my fate, however. I had requested a meeting with Mr. Braithwaite, Chairman of the Interim Advisory Council, who needed to be aware of the position of the funding institutions and my own position as well. It was at this meeting that Mr. Braithwaite stunned me by indicating that in the view of the Council, the Agency for Rural Transformation was doing valuable work and that they would like to see the process continue. Sadly, I had to inform him that my initial reasons and purpose in coming to Grenada had now vanished into thin air and that as a matter of principle I would be unable to stay. Another director of the programme would have to be appointed.

Something else had begun to bother me about Grenada on my return. It was as if that intense and wholly negative experience which had anticlimactically taken place in the space of a few short days, after almost five years of hope, had taken a negative psychological toll on the national spirit. It became difficult to speak even with people who had been friends before the whole fiasco took place because now everyone was wondering whose side the other person was on. Were you a "Coardite" or a "Bishop supporter"? Were you glad the Americans intervened and "saved" Grenada or were you distressed by the fact that your country's sovereignty had been violated? Were you one of those who endorsed the cowardly assassination of Maurice Bishop or were you one who stood for principle and had been jailed in the process? There were now so many tensions in this small society. Even Grenadians were afraid to really speak out about their true feelings. In the midst of all this trauma and tension, there was no room for a non-Grenadian to take an open stance on any of the issues. The country had been torn from limb to limb, virtually.

So anxious I became to pack up and go that I left without some family heirlooms given to me by my mother. Bruised, broken and highly traumatized, I was forced to come to grips with reality (somewhat) some two weeks after my return to Trinidad when Adeline felt she finally needed some answers. "So where," said she, "is the china cabinet?" *(Oh my God!)* "And how about the rocking chair that your father gave me even before your sister was born? *(Oh! My! God!)* "Oh yes, and the little mahogany bed on which you slept as a child?" *(Stop! I have to go back to Grenada. Don't ask me how, but I have to go!)*

This was the start of my understanding of what the experience had done to me. In an effort to block from my consciousness how both my mental and my physical state had been affected, I had taken a blanket decision that I was putting my Grenada house on the market with every stick of furniture, furnishing and equipment it contained, down to the last tiny but useful kitchen accessories. That I could forget the china cabinet in a sense was the most unbelievable since it contained wedding gifts from 1968 which I had had my mother carefully put away and which I subsequently transported to Barbados and then to Grenada. It also contained family heirlooms accumulated by Adeline when she was a young woman, as part of her collection in preparation for marriage. In fact, the cabinet itself was a gift from my father to Adeline, certainly before my sister and I were born. Was I mad? In the months to come, my traumatized state would become evident each time a vehicle back-fired when I would jump out of my skin, as I did when the bombs were falling around me on Old Fort.

In January of 1984, I returned to Grenada in the company of my brother Reginald, on leave from his assignment in Canada and with an earlier plan to spend some of that time with me in Grenada, had things been normal. Before the tragic events unfolded, I had worked so hard at convincing him that what was happening there was good and positive and had finally made a huge dent in his skepticism, a skepticism which Coard and company were ultimately to confirm. Now, he accompanied me by way of protection because those black-lists still existed and how could I know that my name was not on one of them? In the end, I think I was the only foreign national who had worked in Grenada whose name did not appear on the list. He and I spent a few days there, trying to make the best of a sad situation. I made arrangements to have the family heirlooms transported back to Trinidad and we had lunch in the countryside with some friends the day before we left.

My son was never the same after Grenada, no doubt as a result of the terrifying experiences and my lack of awareness that we all should have received psychological counselling. But what did I know of such things? In 1990 the realization hit me with full force when, as a board member of the Trinidad and Tobago Television station whose staff had been held hostage by a group of insurrectionists, I was party to a decision that the entire staff should be the beneficiaries of psychological counselling to help them over the trauma. It was only then, so many years later, that it occurred to me that that is what I should have done. Instead, banking on the natural courage and strength inherited from my mother, I had convinced myself that I could overcome the experience and move on with my life.

I finally turned my attention to settling down in Trinidad and Tobago – the option I had rejected out of hand some years earlier was no easier for me so many years later. I was determined, however, to take the bit between my teeth and do whatever was necessary. At least I was a national of this country and entitled to say my piece.

I was home to stay.

7 ✍ Trinidad 1984-1996

Settling In!

AT THE PERSONAL level, it was the 1960s all over again. Or, it might as well have been since I was back at Park Lane, Tunapuna, living with my mother. Adeline made it clear that, despite her years (and indeed mine), she was the mistress of Park Lane. At the age of 82, this "early feminist" had not by any means changed her approach to life. Curiously, she had lived with me on two occasions in Jamaica and in Barbados and, perhaps because she viewed me as in charge, so to speak, in those contexts, she had displayed attitudes which were altogether docile and conciliatory. Back on home turf, however, Adeline ruled the roost.

I had foolishly thought that, having offered to pay the house-keeper's salary and purchase the food, I would share in the decision making. But while contributions in kind were graciously accepted by Adeline, those of a verbal nature had little impact. I remember once offering to use the rather large tract of land behind the family house to build a home for myself and children, thinking that, as an octogenarian, she would jump at the opportunity to have one of her children and two of her grandchildren so close, in the event of any emergency. Well, my mother let it be understood that this was a decision she would not take without consulting with her other two children. Realizing that this issue was getting rather more compli-cated than I had thought – I honestly believed I was doing her a favour of some kind – I hastily withdrew my offer and began to look around for a house of my own to purchase.

Given that my siblings were resident outside of Trinidad, I chose a location in close proximity to hers, paid the deposit and settled down to furnishing it at my leisure while I continued to live at her house until, possibly, sometime early in 1986. But my mother had her own views on the matter. Casually one day, around September of 1985, she said to me, "So, when are you planning to move?" Stunned at the unexpectedness of the question, I replied, "Uh – well,

I'm not sure – why?" "I'm planning to paint the house in time for Christmas," she said, "and it would make things easier if there were fewer people around." "You are going to *paint* the house for *Christmas?*" was my startled reply. "You didn't tell me." (This said accusingly.) "Oh, but I don't have to tell you everything," she said. "It's my decision to make." Her reply, made calmly enough, had the consequence of sending thunderbolts through my system. I knew that my children and I had to move out.

In August of 1984 the children had joined me from Barbados where they had been living with Frank and we had all settled down to the challenge of living in Trinidad. Challenging, but not boring! Interestingly, and certainly coincidentally, Frank had returned to Trinidad at the same time. The transfer from the Cave Hill to the St. Augustine campus of the University of the West Indies, which he had been requesting for some time, finally had come through. We were both back in Trinidad – Frank accompanied by a new wife; Regina with her memories and her nightmares. The children, once more, had both parents on the same island.

As if managing with the Adeline factor were not enough, I had also been relegated to sharing a bedroom with eight-and-a-half-year-old Lara in my mother's three-bedroom house, the third bedroom naturally having to be given to my son. On an almost weekly basis I would have to tolerate the grumblings of this little girl, complaining that she was not used to sharing a bedroom with anyone, obviously quite oblivious of the fact that the discomfort, if any, was really mine! In retrospect, I can perhaps understand why my mother, a year later, finally had had enough and made it clear that she wanted her old life back. Used to keeping a spotlessly neat home, she was forced to tolerate the spread of 1,000-piece jigsaw puzzles on her living room floor which the children were taking their time to complete, not to mention LEGO cities which my son was building. I remember the day she really blew her top when my daughter and the children next door made real mud cakes on the floor of her verandah. I think she actually made overseas calls to both my brother and sister to complain about this latest offence.

Then there was the issue with the pet dog given to us by my friend, Jenny. Born of a German Shepherd father and a Doberman mother, this dog was already quite large at six months. He pushed open my mother's front gate one day, went for a stroll and was apparently sighted by someone who knew a good thing when he saw it. Under my daughter's loving tutelage, he had grown to think of himself as human, to trust human beings and to treat other dogs as the enemy. Luring him away was therefore little trouble for the young man who abducted and later sold him. The children looked for him everywhere for a full week, distressed beyond measure and finally we gave up. It must have been about three weeks later we heard someone calling at the gate, quite late, one evening. It was the police. They had both perpetrator and dog in their custody and were looking for the owner.

Apparently, the father of the young man who had stolen the dog was a soldier. He noticed that suddenly his son had a great deal of spending money, questioned him as to how he had come by it and eventually the young man broke down and confessed. His father took him to the police who had him lead them to the people who had bought the dog and the dog was taken away in police custody as "stolen goods". The young man had absolutely no idea whose dog he had stolen. However, he knew the general area in which he had found him, and this is what led the police to do a house to house, leading eventually to my mother's house when one of the neighbours indicated that we had lost a dog. I had to go to the police station to identify the dog and agree to appear in court when the case was called. Meanwhile, the police berated me for not reporting the loss of the dog. (*Well, how was I to know that such an action would not be construed as a waste of police time?*) Overjoyed at having the dog returned when all hope had gone, I meekly apologized.

It was my first time in court. Unsure of what to expect, but confident that I would be there for a long time, I had brought along a book to read. Not the done thing, it seems. I was gently tapped on the shoulder by the officer on duty and told that such action was deemed to be showing disrespect for the court. I folded my arms, waited and watched the ebb and flow of human traffic in the courtroom. Proceedings began on time and in a fairly low-key yet professional manner. This was a magistrates' court so I suppose no pomp and ceremony was to be expected. The case involving my dog was third in line. The young man was brought forward and the charges against him read, after which the magistrate asked him, kindly, "Is there anyone here in court for you today?" My heart almost broke for him as he looked around the courtroom, with a combination of anticipation and despair, then turned to the magistrate and mutely shook his head. Frankly, I almost stood up for him at that point.

I had met him the week before when I went to the police station to identify the dog and the police had asked if I wanted to meet him. I did and in fact ended up buying him a chicken dinner because he looked so hungry and so miserable. He could not have been more than sixteen or seventeen. What could have gone wrong, especially if your father is a soldier, for heaven's sake? The police teased me a bit when I brought back the meal for him, but allowed him to have it. Sentence was passed and I was allowed to collect my dog which was still being held in police custody as evidence.

When for the second time some months later this giant of a dog disappeared, I knew exactly what I had to do. And I hit pay dirt. Apparently, this second abductor was very clever. He took the dog, yes, but he also went to the police and gave a statement that he had found this dog bearing such and such a description in such and such a location. He had thus discharged his civic responsibility and had I acted the way I did the first time, the dog would have been his for keeps and his conscience clear. For the second time, the dog was rescued.

At the professional level, this early 1984 re-immersion into Trinidad society had been facilitated by the fact that CUSO Internatoinal, the Canadian development agency mentioned earlier, appointed me one of two programme investigators to travel to Belize, Jamaica and the Leeward Islands to review projects, meet with groups, identify possibilities for funding and make recommendations for CUSO's upcoming five-year programme. This consultancy, which took me the better part of three months, also gave me the opportunity to continue with my regional development work (I had been appointed Interim Coordinator of CARIPEDA) and I timed my travel to return via Barbados where I spent the Easter vacation with the children who had been living there with Frank since our Grenada departure.

Belize was the highlight of this trip. Knowing that the CUSO programming favoured indigenous peoples, I asked my local contacts to arrange for me not merely to visit a Mayan community but to spend some time with them. The idea was that this would allow me the opportunity to begin to understand their lifestyle and their needs so that I could more credibly present my proposals on their behalf. It was a wonderful experience and one I will never forget. Indeed, this was the starting point of my plan for how I decided I would spend the rest of my life after I had taken care of child raising.

Located in a setting designed by nature herself, the dwellings of

*I meet with Mayan farmers in Belize during
the CUSO programme investigation*

the Maya village comprised split log walls, dirt floors and thatched roofs. Simplicity of lifestyle does not even begin to describe it. Cooking was done at a fireplace while the food itself was basic but nutritious. I think that, as the one concession to modernity, there was a transistor radio, but nothing more. I left the community with a clear vision for my future in mind. The eco-retreat which I subsequently established and currently manage began to take shape as a result of this visit.

By November of 1984, I had had enough of international travelling and consultancies and started to look for a regular job. Challenges immediately posed themselves. Teaching, for obvious reasons, was out of the question. Work in a government office was equally impracticable, since working in the NGO development field had made me so critical of governmental systems that it would have been an act of hypocrisy to now become party to said systems. I checked the newspapers daily and consulted with friends. Eventually, I was presented with what I thought was an opportunity that I felt I could not refuse.

It seemed that the government, in some areas, was attempting to act more responsibly and, for example, had decided to establish a state enterprise dedicated to the coordination, management and control of non-traditional products for export. It was set up as a statutory body headed by a chief executive officer and board of directors which had full control over the process. Formal commencement of these operations was set for January 1985. It was to this company that I applied and was hired in the post of senior research officer with effect from its starting date.

I really ought to have known better. I ought to have known that anything with a public sector stamp on it would not give me the satisfaction I had experienced in the NGO sector. What began for me as an opportunity I saw to make a difference, to help create new wealth among small craft and other producers turned into a nightmare of wastage, both of time and money, of pomp and ceremony signifying nothing, really. There were fancy offices and cubicles, secretaries to wait on managers, uniformed staff to serve tea at intervals, all within a brand new building with its own private underground parking. Quickly I became both bored and frustrated.

But this was not all. I had purchased a vehicle on my return to Trinidad and directed my mind to the task of learning to drive all over again, Trinidad not conforming to any of the situations I had encountered in any other place I had lived. Why, for heaven's sake, was there *always* so much traffic on the roads? Why was everyone *always* in such a hurry? Why were they *always* so impatient? So, when in January of 1985 I began to work in Port of Spain, I cut quite a figure of fun to my friends by leaving my car parked at home and taking the bus. This arrangement worked fine for me, helping me to avoid the monstrous traffic to which I was unaccustomed – until the rainy season came. Tired of being splashed with dirty water by insensitive motorists and waiting for long periods while the flood waters on the streets of Port of Spain subsided, I decided that I had paid my dues. I backtracked and began to drive to work. It did not help either that I was assigned to work with a consultant from Australia with whom I made frequent field visits to rural projects. His favourite saying was that the shortest possible time between any two points was a traffic light in Trinidad changing to green and the sounding of a motorist's horn. His joke always irritated me, especially as he thought it was very funny; but I knew it to be true since the motorists kept proving him correct time and again.

Further Settling In Problems!

The distress signals for me continued to mount, however, principally with regard to features of the society at large which I had great difficulty getting used to. Chief among these was the emphasis on materialism. At the start of the 1980s the oil boom was declared over, yet in the mid to late eighties many continued to flaunt wealth as if it were very much a thing of the present, oblivious of what the future might hold. My daughter, for instance, complained to me that she was the only one in her prep school class who did not have at least $20 spending money daily. In fact, she said, some children had $100 bills. She was embarrassed, she said, at the fact that I gave her only $3 which could only buy a small drink and a snack. "But what more do you need?" I wanted to know. "I give you breakfast before you leave home and pack a hot lunch for you with a flask of juice. The $3 spending money is merely meant to introduce you to the *practice* of spending money since one can't get through life without doing it at some stage!" Not at all convinced by my argument, she sulked until I raised the daily allowance to $5. Not surprisingly, neither in Barbados nor in Grenada had the amount of spending money ever been an issue.

Imagine my further surprise when one afternoon she came home from school brandishing a cheque from the Ministry of Education – a cheque which represented the payment of a book grant. Here she was, attending a privately run preparatory school and being the recipient of a grant for the purchase of school books. Where was the logic? If a parent is prepared to pay what in those days was the princely sum of $600 a term for a child's tuition, surely that parent is able to afford the books! My son, by the way, also came home with a cheque, larger than his sister's since he was attending secondary school. This was somewhat more understandable given that his was a public school and questions of discrimination could be raised if all the students were not recipients of cheques.

Another distressing experience for me was the fact that I now no longer recognized nor was I recognized by anyone in my home town of Tunapuna. I would walk up and down the Eastern Main Road, visit the side streets, including those close to my mother's house and fail to recognize anyone! My trips to the market on Saturdays lost most of their appeal for this reason. Gone was the opportunity to see old school mates and catch up on what had happened in between – jobs, marriage, children. I think in the space of time that I spent in Tunapuna and later on, in Tacarigua, I encountered only three such people. Petty though it might sound, it was experiences such as these that intensified my distress and discomfort at being forced to return to live in the society from which for several years I had felt alienated. In contrast, and encouragingly, my mother's friendships were all intact. These women, all in their eighties, had kept their relationships firmly in place over the years. In honour and appreciation of them all, I threw a surprise party in 1987 to celebrate Adeline's 85th birthday. And they all came!

Politics in Trinidad and Tobago in the Mid-1980s

A possible opportunity to shake up what had become an attitude of "money is no problem, so we can spend as we like" came at the time of the 1986 general election when the political party which had held power for 30 consecutive years was defeated by an overwhelming majority. Of the 36 seats contested they won a mere three. The winning party comprised a mix of separate parties which had formed themselves into a single alliance, convinced that this was the only way to win against the party which had dominated the scene for such a long time. Interestingly, A.N.R. Robinson, the politician who had been selected to head this party, was a native of Tobago, the tiny sister island of the twin-island state of Trinidad and Tobago. In the mere five years in which he led the country, Tobago benefitted via the establishment of an international airport, the dredging of the Scarborough harbour and pier extension – projects which had commenced under the previous administration but which were completed under the auspices of the man from Tobago. A number of economic measures were also introduced, no doubt as a means of counteracting the negative fallout and impact which the country was experiencing (albeit unconsciously) following its reversal in oil fortunes.

Here in sum was a nation, accustomed to being pampered by its politicians, now led by one – a Tobagonian at that – who was attempting to be responsible by reducing or removing altogether the tax allowances and perquisites which, over the years, the populace had become used to enjoying as a matter of course. To add insult to injury, a value added tax was introduced which placed an additional 15 percent on the cost of what were considered non-essential purchases. In attempting to shield his country from the potential ravages of multilateral institutions like the International Monetary Fund, the Prime Minister made a lot of enemies for himself. Within his own party and after less than two years in government, a break-away faction calling itself Club 88 emerged, subsequently becoming a separate political party, but not before the devastating Jamaat al Muslimeen intervention in 1990 which all but caused this new government to collapse.

In July of 1990, 114 members of this Muslim organization stormed the Red House, the seat of Parliament, and took the Prime Minister and his Cabinet hostage while other members of the organization attacked the only television station in existence at the time and one of the two radio stations. It surprised no one therefore, that the then Opposition party, which had lost ninety per cent of the electoral seats only five years earlier, managed to wrest power from this fledgling and divided unit and resume the reins of government. Politics and economics – a volatile mix. Less than five years after being re-elected in 1991 by a populace which had spurned them in 1986, the new government called a snap election that ended with results in Trinidad that were tied with those of the opposition.

Interestingly, it was the self-same embattled former Tobagonian prime minister whose party had won the two Tobago seats, a party which had no links to either the then government or the opposition, who broke the tie. He decided to align his two seats with those of the opposition, thus giving a third party, in as many terms, a shot at administering the affairs of the country. One should also add as a footnote that the former official opposition with whom the former prime minister was now joining forces represented the core of the breakaway faction of his coalition party in 1988.

I was one of those who thought, in 1986, that a new administration would bring a new approach to the culture by which the country had been run for so many years. Maybe, if time and the electorate had permitted it, this might have happened. However, in the overall scheme of things, five years is not such a long time, especially if one wants to reverse attitudes and practices which have run long and deep. I remained in my state sector job for three years, always hoping that things would improve and finally left at the end of 1987. I had journeyed to the far reaches of the island to meet and interact with people, arranging for samples of their work to be collected. I had talked my CEO into allowing me to extend my CUSO trips to Canada to investigate markets for the products I knew our small entrepreneurs were producing successfully. I had written reports with recommendations for follow-up action and even managed to do some sample shipments of craft items. All to no avail.

However, it was not merely at the level of public administration that things remained unchanged and continued to frustrate me. The issue of respect for the environment, despite at least one government campaign that comes to mind, remained somewhere outside of the consciousness of the country's citizens. I recall one very rainy day, shortly after moving into my townhouse behind which ran a deep drain, hearing strange noises which appeared to be coming from that general location. I strolled outside to have a look and the spectacle which met my eyes will remain in my memory forever. There, crashing through the drain, moved along by the heavy torrent of water, were toys, old appliances, bags of garbage, tyres, discarded pieces of furniture.

Puzzled, because I had never seen anything like this before, I stood gaping at the sight when my neighbour, a young man of about 25, approached the drain with a bag filled with garbage and calmly tossed it into the mix. "What are you doing?!" I shrieked at him, unable to help myself. "Throwing away the garbage," he replied patiently, as if addressing a not so bright adolescent. "The drain will wash it down to the river." Then it struck me. The idea behind his and the other people's method of waste disposal, clearly in use over several years, was simply to remove the garbage from *their* immediate environs. What happened to it subsequently was none of their concern. That was the thinking – and still is, unfortunately, in many instances. Interestingly, that was the year when the Caroni River in Central Trinidad overflowed its banks and effectively, for at least twelve hours, cut off access between the north of the country and the south. The Caura River, a tributary of the Caroni, was the river into which all these bags of garbage and other items would be deposited via that drain which ran behind my home.

To its credit, the 1986 administration appointed a cabinet minister with responsibility for the environment, inter alia. However, the prime minister subsequently demonstrated that votes were more important to him than saving the environment when he later fired this minister who had suggested that the government take legal issue with those persons who consistently set fires in the northern range of mountains as a means of facilitating their slash and burn approaches to land clearance.

Birth of a New Regional NGO:
My Role As Midwife and Wet Nurse

At the end of 1987, I received an offer to manage the Caribbean Network for Integrated Rural Development (CNIRD), a regional NGO with a focus on rural development. Interestingly, the offer had come from my former boss with whom I had worked at the Caribbean Conference of Churches. Completely fed up by then with the lacklustre approach to people development by the agency with which I was employed, I merely asked that I be given a few days to consult with my children and discuss the opportunity with them. I wanted that job! I was certain that this would allow me to make the contributions to both the national and regional communities which my position within the state sector enterprise surely could not offer. Consultation with the children was important given that the new job would require a fair amount of travelling and it was important that I have their cooperation and consent since I always tried to have us work as a team.

Adeline, when I told her about leaving my state sector job and assuming this one, made it clear, without saying it in so many words, that she thought I was being irresponsible. She said something akin to, "Don't forget you have two children to take care of..." and left the reminder sort of hanging grimly in the air. Boldly I soldiered on. I had not been through the ravages of a Grenadian experience only to emerge a coward at the end of it all. Moreover, I disliked intensely my current job and loved the promise that this one held for me.

Actually, it was more than a promise because I had been given the authority to move the programme along as I saw fit, once I stayed within the broad parameters of its organizational objectives. The really scary part, which I have saved for last, is that the programme, at the time I assumed my position, had a total in funds of just about US$10,000. I would have to single-handedly raise the capital to operate it. The experience of a development worker, however, prepares one for taking risk and this challenge I was prepared to shoulder wholeheartedly. Moreover, although at the time I could not know this, it would serve me in good stead years later in my entrepreneurial development phase of life.

Oddly enough, the idea for the establishment of the CNIRD, was born out of a joint university/public sector/NGO recognition that while their individual sectors were doing a great deal for rural communities throughout the region, impact was limited given the absence of either formal or informal linkages and cooperation between and among them. The rationale for such a network to be established was that it would create a strategy by which government, non-government, community-based and university agencies and practitioners would, where applicable, combine their human and other resources to work together to achieve positive results for their rural communities. Such collaboration would help promote and strengthen rural development initiatives with a view to transforming the rural sectors via appropriate socio-economic initiatives. It was agreed that such networking and collaboration would take place both at the local level in the individual countries as well as within the regional sphere. In the late 1980s, it was viewed as an idea whose time had come.

Regional NGO Politics Rears Its Head!

Since the CNIRD was a new organization, my first task was to communicate its existence to the region as well as obtain feedback on programme content and support for the effort. At the administrative level funds had to be raised internationally for its continuation. The latter turned out to be far easier to achieve than the former. I was already acquainted with most of the NGO development projects, programmes and stakeholders in the region and therefore assumed that the organization I was promoting would be readily and easily accepted, based on trust if nothing else. I was in for a surprise, however. Suddenly I was viewed with suspicion and a great deal of questioning which really had me quite puzzled until a fellow development worker from Dominica explained what the problem really was.

It appears that I had gained a reputation, while in Grenada, for raising large sums of money for development projects and while that was acceptable in the Grenadian context, it became a challenge now that I was representing a regional organization. Ultimately, the fear was that, by gaining funding support for CNIRD, I would, in essence, be depriving their agencies of what they would otherwise have received, were CNIRD not in the picture.

Having worked with funding agencies both in Geneva and Barbados, I knew there was no truth to this belief. Projects are funded on the basis of worth – "worth" being understood as value within the context in which they were to be applied and trust in the institutions responsible for their implementation. If it meant expanding their budgets to the particular country or region, these agencies were usually prepared to do so. But I could not give up.

Fairly easily I had achieved the support of the state agencies. I simply had to work harder and more consistently at attaining that of my NGO partners. Support from the University of the West Indies was unquestionable. Not only was I granted free office space on the St. Augustine campus, but I continuously received support and guidance from those UWI representatives who sat on the management committee. Indeed, the co-chairpersons of this committee each headed the UWI Department to which they were attached: So it was that P. I. Gomes was Head of the Department of Agricultural Extension at UWI, St. Augustine, Trinidad and Geoff Brown was Head of the Social Welfare Training Centre at the Department of Social Services at UWI, Mona, Jamaica.

CNIRD's Contribution to Caribbean Rural Development

One year later, in December of 1988, the CNIRD was launched at a General Assembly convened at the St. Augustine campus of the University of the West Indies. This first meeting was crucial. Participation was drawn from national, regional and international non-governmental organizations; regional inter-governmental institutions; national governmental institutions; as well as national and community-based grassroots organizations. Participants were not merely required to listen to the proposal and the rationale for the establishment of what could have been viewed as yet another regional institution. They were also being asked to determine its importance and the singular role it could play by charting further paths based on the realities within the region. Without the deliberation, blessing and support of these organizations, there would have been no programme either designed or implemented to push things forward.

As it turned out, the response was unanimous. Not only was there collective approval for the establishment of the CNIRD but clear programme areas were also defined at the assembly. It was agreed that there should be five main programmes: Information Networking, Research, Training, Exchanges and Advocacy, all with a view to improving the lives of those in the rural sectors throughout the Caribbean. The strategy to be utilized to plan, develop and implement these programming areas would be that of networking. Its

Workshop planning in Dominica

geographic span ranged from Belize in Central America to Guyana in South America and with the inclusion of the Dominican Republic in the northern Caribbean zone. It was an ambitious programme, requiring a structure which needed to be both efficient and reliable.

This first General Assembly immediately identified and appointed a management committee comprising a team of regional organizations which would oversee the CNIRD in the intervening periods between general assemblies which would be held every three years. The main purpose of the General Assembly would therefore be to determine progress and chart further paths forward based on realities within the region. The management committee consisted of two representatives from the University of the West Indies (UWI). In addition, there was representation from the Caribbean Community (CARICOM) Secretariat, the Caribbean People's Development Agency (CARIPEDA), the Caribbean Policy Development Centre (CPDC), the Caribbean Conservation Association (CCA), the Caribbean Association for Feminist Research and Action (CAFRA) and the Windward Islands Farmers' Association (WINFA). Here altogether was a cross section of rural development interests and sectors whose representatives were constantly in touch with their rural grassroots bases throughout the region.

To ensure that there was no top-down development and planning taking place, CNIRD was represented in each country by a delegate. Sometimes it was an NGO representative, at other times a government official, but always someone community based whose task it was to organize Local Development Agencies (LDAs). They were expected to respond to national rural community develop-ment needs and initiatives in their respective countries. It was the responsibility of CNIRD to facilitate the efforts of these local networks inclusive of programme financing at both the local and the regional levels. Regarding practical on-the-ground tasks in which national partners were engaging, the expertise of the Carib-bean Agricultural Regional Development Institute (CARDI) and the Inter-American Institute for Cooperation in Agriculture (IICA) as well as the Food and Agricultural Organization (FAO) were regularly utilized. Indeed, in many cases they formed part of the LDA membership.

By 1992 the information networking programme had launched INCARD – the Information Network for Caribbean Rural Develop-ment – a documentation service developed in collaboration with the United Nations Economic Commission for Latin America and the Caribbean (ECLAC). INCARD published *Network News* which gave regular updates of abstracted rural development material obtain-able from CNIRD's own computerized database. Given that CNIRD was linked by modem to ECLAC, we were also able to obtain and disseminate additional information from this second valuable source to national and regional NGOs which would normally not be in communication with such a large inter-governmental institu-tion. The information networking programme did not stop there, however, launching as it did a series of publications geared towards informing the regional and international communities on various aspects of integrated rural development appropriate to the region. Such publications ranged from who's who directories to a cartoon booklet on the handling and application of agrochemicals to a regional newsletter, *Rural Link-up,* all of which were extremely well received.

The research programme undertook studies on land reform in the Windward Islands and the information collected was disseminated not only as a regional study but also as country monographs and fact sheets. Additionally, research was done in the areas of market-ing, diversification within the banana industry and the socio-economic status of rural youth in the Caribbean. The highlight of the exchanges programme was a workshop organized in November

of 1991 by CNIRD and IICA which brought together key government and non-government agents in the region to establish a rural
development strategy for the area. This decision was later ratified by
the Standing Committee of Ministers of Agriculture in the region.

I think one of the most amazing revelations of my rural development career – and the CNIRD experience amply bore this out – was
the recognition that rural dwellers, though mostly underserved if
not ignored by both the mainstream and successive administrations,
are always aware of what they need in order to make their lives
meaningful. They also know their capabilities and how, if enhanced,
these capabilities could work to their benefit ultimately. Infrastructural needs almost always played a huge role in their suggested lists
of requirements. Farmers were always clamouring for feeder roads,
fishermen for refrigeration facilities, youth for sporting facilities,
communities for schools. The lists displayed a remarkable resem-
blance in content, no matter which country they came from.

The CNIRD advocacy programme thus tended to focus on high-
lighting and publicizing these needs, using the power and authority of the network to get the word out to the relevant government
authority to provide them. Additionally, funds were raised from
overseas sources and provided to the community via the local
networks which acted as project coordinators.

Creative Linkages Help Develop the CNIRD Programme

CNIRD formed many linkages with other organizations, these
tending to be formal rather than casual. It was agreed that networking would be the official approach and programming strategy for
the organization. The Commonwealth Foundation, the NGO arm of
the Commonwealth Secretariat, was one such creative linkage that
presented itself. Not only did it allow for the opportunity to travel
to parts of the Commonwealth I would have been unable to visit,
but also many useful experiences were enjoyed, and ideas obtained
through direct exchanges with persons and projects from the many
different cultures. In addition, plans for my Retreat, in the organizational and planning stages at the time, were given the opportunity to emerge and take shape in my mind's eye.

This Foundation held an NGO Forum every four years, preceding that of the Commonwealth Heads of Government Meeting
(CHOGM) with a view to having the views of NGOs from throughout
the Commonwealth feed into the discussions of the Commonwealth

Heads. Much planning and consultation would go into the preparations for these meetings and would be facilitated via the establishment of a task force. In practice, the task force was appointed well in advance of the event to discuss the various themes of the agenda and mechanisms for ensuring that the networks of NGOs in all the countries of the Commonwealth had the opportunity for input. It was an excellent example of networking in action.

The Harare NGO Forum, held in 1991, gave me the opportunity to travel to southern Africa and to visit a country, Zimbabwe, in which like most of us from this part of the world I had enormous interest. I remember feeling a sense of disillusionment when journeying into the rural areas, since I didn't have the impression that much development had taken place on behalf of those who had struggled so hard for their freedom. I had just been reading a book entitled *Mothers of the Revolution* by Caroline Rooney, in which the struggles of the black Zimbabwean population, of women in particular, had been described in detail. It was difficult to imagine that President Mugabe could have come to power in Zimbabwe in 1980 without grassroots support. Eleven years later, on my visit to the country, the anticipation of visible and tangible benefits to his people seemed reasonable to me. Unfortunately, while the capital Harare could rival that of almost any metropolitan country, the rural areas provided little to fulfill expectations in this regard.

In 1992, once more under the auspices of the Commonwealth Foundation, came the opportunity to visit Kuala Lumpur, Malaysia. This was my first trip to a strictly Muslim country, and I was riveted by the voice of the flight attendant who outlined very clearly before the plane landed the many forms of prosecution and punishment in store for those who broke the law by indulging in substances considered illegal in that country. The social highlight of the trip was my meeting with one of the group who had been in Estonia with me in 1982. She was Malaysian and was attending the Forum as a local delegate. Over the years we had kept in touch and I had contacted her when I knew I was going to be in Kuala Lumpur. She did not hesitate to seek me out and take me sightseeing as we both relived our three-week stay in Estonia so many years earlier.

Returning to the hotel where I was staying after she had taken me to visit a museum, she suddenly realized that she had left her camera behind. To my utter amazement, she took a small phone out of her bag, dialed a number, spoke to someone who ascertained that

Meeting with my Malaysian friend after ten years!

her camera was safe, and we returned to fetch it. This was 1992 and the concept of a mobile phone was one I had certainly never heard of, but here was my friend using this accessory as if it were the most normal thing in the world.

NGOs and Financial Independence

Looking back at the responsibility of managing an NGO, one issue which had dogged me ever since my Grenada initiation had to do with income generation. Partner agencies in the region had spent many sessions discussing this but ultimately, we continued to be dependent on the generosity of the international donors. In an effort to begin the process of change in this regard, as Director of the Agency for Rural Transformation (ART) in Grenada, I had instituted a policy whereby 6 per cent of all funds raised for projects would be paid to ART as an administration fee. Some international agencies immediately saw the value of this approach and applauded it while others were not so sure. The idea, however, was that over time these funds would accumulate in a special account with a view to presenting ART with the opportunity to invest in an income-generating project which would defray at least some of the Agency's expenses.

Thanks to those responsible for destroying the Grenada revolutionary process, this idea never had the opportunity to get off the ground but it did stay with me. In 1990/91 came the opportunity for CNIRD to become involved in an investment project which, if properly financed and managed, could spell nothing but financial success for the organization. A member of the organization's management committee was selling a building in St. Augustine at what can only be described as a bargain price. St. Augustine, being a university town, is clearly prime real estate given that student accommodation would always be in demand. The idea was to convert the building located on the property into a student residential facility with a small cafeteria attached. However, CNIRD could not on its own generate the cash required to pay for the building and renovations and sought the partnership of another regional organization with which we had a good working relationship. In fact, they had representation on our management committee.

Imagine my disappointment and surprise when the request for partnering was turned down on the ground that one could not be sure what would happen in respect of the assets should the venture fail. There had been no question of consideration of the cash flow projections which had been prepared, of discussion of a management and administrative structure to oversee the operations, of a system for regular evaluations. Instead, they had literally thrown the baby out with the bathwater. The project had to be shelved because CNIRD could not go it alone. In a sense, this experience was perhaps a good thing for it made me more resolved than ever to demonstrate to myself and the NGO community that development principles could be profitably applied to entrepreneurial development. Now I was certain that I would be definitely embarking on my own project.

Single Parenting and Its Challenges!

The challenges for me were, however, not confined to what was happening on the job. On the home front, many changes were taking place. The children had both become adolescents and I remember when Janine Omolara, my daughter, turned 13 in 1988 and I could thereafter tell people with pride that I had two teenage children. Little did I realize, however, that this reality in effect presented its own challenges. Finally, I began to empathize with the difficulties my mother would have had to face in raising her children single-handedly, especially Regina, the rebel. The trouble was that I was torn between not wanting to be the overprotective mother

that I had resented having, while recognizing the need to be responsible in fulfilling my role. Communication, I thought, was the single
most important key to this but while it worked with my daughter, it
had no effect whatsoever on my son.

I would regularly call little family meetings for us to discuss
issues – travel or other plans which I had, decisions regarding their
welfare which I was in the process of taking but wanting their
opinion, possible issues which they might want to share with me.
Janine Omolara (we called her Lara) participated fully while Frank
Ayodele merely mumbled, when pressed. It seems, however, that
he communicated on a regular basis with his sister who, fiercely
loyal to him, only let me in on the tidbits determined by her to be
germane to any given matter.

There was, for example, the time I was sure I smelled an illegal
substance in his room and confronted him about it. His was a
mumbled denial which left me nowhere really, since I found no
evidence to support my suspicion. Well, the next day, and in his
absence, I was thoroughly taken to task by Lara who asked me if I
didn't realize how much her brother disliked any association with
that substance and how could I possibly have made such an accu-
sation? Defensively, I had to remind her that I could not possibly
know that he felt that way since communication with me did not
appear to be at the top of his list!

Parenting! That most difficult of all tasks! One never knows if one
is on the right track and in the end it is the child, as an adult, who
decides the path to be followed. I have never defined myself in terms
of motherhood, however, but rather as a person, a professional who
also happens to be a mother and must take those responsibilities
equally seriously. Looking back at the way that I and others of my
acquaintance parented and the various endings that resulted, I am
now convinced that the role of parents is to do the best possible
with regard to the caring and comfort within one's reach, a decent
education, good health and sound moral values. What is important,
in my view, is that the child should be able to admit, as an adult,
that the parent(s) did the best that they could as parent(s), recognizing that the rest was really up to the child.

As if in subtle recognition of this, one year on Mother's Day Lara
presented me with a "Mother of the Year" award – something she
had bought and filled in the relevant spaces with my name and the
year of presentation. It became a family joke when, some weeks

later, complaining to her brother about some "misdemeanour" on my part, he said to her, "Don't complain to me. You are the one who gave her the 'Mother of the Year' award!" – clear implication that he would never have been so foolhardy as to present such an award!

Challenges at the personal level too!

This was also the period in which I found myself searching for completion of self, I guess one might term it. Something was clearly missing from my existence and I needed to determine what it was. There was an emptiness, a feeling that something more was required. Although I knew that the feeling was not religion based, I tried going back to church – the Good Shepherd Anglican Church. Here I had attended Sunday school and won prizes for good attendance and reciting the *Collect* by heart. Here I had been confirmed, taken communion on a regular basis and, finally, recited my marriage vows. I was supposed to feel at home here. But I didn't; and this despite (or maybe because of?) the fact that nothing had changed over the years regarding the order of service and the hymn singing. Even some of the original choir members were still here, after a 16-year absence on my part. Clearly, this was not what my inner self was seeking.

I shared this dilemma with select persons and most of them tried to help me. I was introduced to the School of Philosophy, an organization which was sort of spiritually based but with a strong practical element to it. Uh-Uh. This was not giving me what I wanted either. Then, one day someone, herself a member of the School of Philosophy, suggested that I try Raja Yoga. Raja Yoga? What is that? Not really explaining to me what it was, she directed me to a centre that, oddly enough, was quite close to where I lived but I had never noticed it before then.

Within the first five minutes of the teacher explaining to me the principles of Raja Yoga, I knew this was what I had been searching for. I felt open, creative and energetic, ready to consider and embrace new perspectives on life and living. This was when I discovered that the Hindu philosophy to which I had been introduced in 1965–66 in the UWI survey course Comparative Religion had never been forgotten. But it was more than that. The comparative studies of those great religions had, in essence, put me in touch with the meaning and essential spirit behind them all and it now awakened in me a sense of spirituality as opposed to religiosity in my approach to life. The teachings of Raja Yoga, for example, opened up my mind to life approaches, the most important of which, practised by me till this day, is the principle of detachment. It is a principle that, if understood and applied, has the power to free mind, spirit and body from human and material inducements which often attract negative results.

Certainly, this new approach to life played a key role, not merely in releasing me from old and unrewarding habits but also in helping me raise my children which I now had to do, practically single-handedly, since in 1989 Frank had departed these shores to assume what he considered to be a more fulfilling academic career in the United States. He kept in touch regularly and the children spent each summer vacation with him. Still, this was not always easy. In 1992, I went on a fund-raising assignment to Europe leaving Lara and her brother at home without any adult supervision. She was after all a sixth-former and her brother was 21.

Naturally, I phoned home frequently to ensure that things were going all right. The last call I made was from Germany after which I would be going to Switzerland, a visit about which I was really excited. It was going to be the first time I would be returning there since leaving in 1976. All plans to meet and greet, professionally and socially had been made, the highlight of my trip being a reunion with Julio de Santa Ana, my former mentor.

Call it maternal intuition if you will, but something struck me as odd in Lara's manner during the phone call that I made from Germany and I knew I needed to get home. Sadly, but definitively, I cancelled my further travel plans and returned home on the earliest flights I could find. All seemed normal on my return and nothing was ever found to be amiss, but I have never felt regret for my decision although it cost me the only opportunity I have ever had to return to Switzerland.

In raising the children, I had tried to ensure that gender balance was applied, bearing in mind the age factor (Frank Ayodele was four years older, a fact which Lara appeared to forget quite frequently). Thus, the bathroom they both shared had to be cleaned, in turn, by both of them; likewise, dishes had to be washed in turn. Both had to help me weed the yard and mow the lawn. Lastly, when they were old enough for me to do without a household helper, we all took turns cleaning the house. There were no "male" or "female" jobs. There were simply jobs in which everyone had to participate.

I was determined that Frank Ayodele would make a husband par excellence one day, with the ability to do everything that was required in a household. Lara, on the other hand, should have the independence of mind and spirit that would disallow dependence on a husband to undertake certain "male" chores.

I was to wonder at the wisdom of this approach one afternoon when I was giving my daughter, her boyfriend and another friend a lift to the cinema. In an effort to make light conversation, I teasingly said to the boyfriend, "So, Marcus, you have to have a fat wallet this afternoon. You have to pay for *three* people." "Not really, Ms. Dumas," replied Marcus. "Lara never allows me to pay for her – she always pays for herself!" Stunned, I looked at my daughter who said, rather defensively, "Well, isn't that the way you raised me? To be independent?" *(Yes, but I didn't think you would take it* that *far!)*

Then there was the time in 1993 that Chez, my soon-to-be second husband, and I were invited by Frank Ayodele to have lunch at his home. He was now living on his own and had a girlfriend to whom he wished to introduce us. Imagine my surprise when I saw this young woman actually *putting* the lunch on his plate for him! Clearing my throat in preparation to offer the helpful explanation that such an action was unnecessary, given that he had been raised to help himself, I felt a prod from beneath the table. Obviously aware, from my body language, of what I was about to do, I was being silently warned by Chez to desist. After we left he asked me if I could not see how happy Frank Ayodele had been to have his lunch dished out for him by someone else!

Perhaps in some ways this approach did work. The mother of my son's children would later tell me that he would rise each morning and prepare the children's lunches for them to take to school, the way I did, he told her. And on occasion I saw him ironing their school uniforms. My daughter, likewise, should her husband's job necessitate that he be away from home for days, would energetically and efficiently play the role of single parent in his absence. In fact, time and again, she has proved herself to be the most organized person I know!

Caring for Adeline – A Reversal of Roles!

As for Adeline, since as early as 1991, she was slowly beginning to show those signs of old age and dementia, although her original spirit of independence remained intact. It was the Christmas of

1991 and I was unwrapping the present which she had given to me. There inside the package lay the Swiss-embroidered tablecloth and napkins which I had purchased for her in Geneva back in 1974. Puzzled, I looked at her and said, "But this is what I gave you several years ago!" "So?..." she retorted, without batting an eyelid. "It's mine and I can give it to whomever I want!" What was I to say? I accepted my present and have had it in safekeeping all these years, thinking of her each time I use the set.

It was the following year that I received a call from her one evening at around 10 o'clock. She had fallen and injured her head. Lara and I jumped into the car and rushed to her home where she still lay on the floor unable to get up because by then she had had both knee and hip surgery. It appeared that after she had eaten her supper, she fell asleep at the table and, while sleeping, had fallen sideways onto the floor, hitting her head at the edge of the table in the process. Lara, unable to stand the sight of blood, shrieked and grabbed hold of me. Not ever having had to tend to any such injury in the case of my children, here I was now confronted with the task of helping my own mother with blood streaming from her head. Well, it was Adeline, the nurse, who took charge of things. Calmly, she instructed me to find where the injury was, to take a pair of scissors, sterilize them and cut the hair off around where the scalp had split. Then she instructed me how to dress it.

After this incident, we knew that she had to have a night nurse and this was quickly taken care of. The night nurse took over as soon as the day worker left and so she was never alone. But then another issue arose. People needed to have time off so I decided to hire a third person who would do weekends only. This lady, Judy was her name, announced that she had had geriatric training and experience and we agreed to give it a try – that is until she made the cardinal error of telling Adeline that she could not enter her own kitchen and certainly could not light the stove because it was dangerous for her to do so. Adeline was decidedly outraged.

Chez and I, by then married, arrived on that Sunday morning from the market to deliver her weekly goods to hear her shouting – something I had rarely heard in all the years I had spent with her. "What's the matter?" I asked. "Do you know this woman?" she said. "Yes, I do. This is Judy." "Well," she said, "in that case, since you know her, *you* take her – I don't want her here!" It took well over an hour to smooth things over, and for Chez to get Judy to apologize and promise not to repeat this heinous offense before Adeline would agree that she could stay. But it was becoming more and more obvious to my brother and me that we would finally have to admit her to a nursing home where she would receive specialized and constant care and attention. We began to do our research.

The notion of trust also reared its head. Seniors who have been used to being in charge, certainly of their own lives, clearly experience issues of distrust when forced to surrender their authority – even to the children whom they have bred and with whose track record they should be well acquainted. When it became clear that my mother was faltering, badly – unaware of where she had put her pension cheques, unable to sign her name properly, not sure of who was in the house with her – I took a decision to take over the control of her finances. I chose a time when I thought she was in clear-thinking mode and discussed my plan with her. To my surprise, she agreed immediately so I put the plan into action at once, taking over her bank books and telling all concerned that in future I would write the cheques and pay the bills.

It was the very next morning that I received a frenzied call from her, asking whether I had taken away her bank books and why?? Caught by surprise, I did my best to explain by reminding her that we had had a conversation about it the day before. To no avail, however. But, as if this were not bad enough, I then received two separate calls from my siblings who wanted to know what was going on. She had called them and complained about my "misdemeanour" and they were taking me to task, albeit politely. Words cannot explain how I felt. I left for work, went immediately to her home and handed her the bank books, determined now to leave her to her own devices. But, how could I? She was my mother and although I could not understand the entirety of what was happening to her, I knew she needed help – help which I had to do my best to give, never mind we did not share the same household.

Dealing with senility and dementia when it affects your loved ones is one of the most difficult challenges for anyone to undertake. In a sense, I had begun to prepare for it some years earlier based on the experience of one of my friends. Her mother, a woman in her sixties, had been diagnosed with Alzheimer's disease and the symptoms, introduced to me for the first time, were distressing to say the least. Imagine not recognizing your husband of some 40 years! Or the very children you have birthed and reared! "Who is this man in my bedroom?" my friend's mother wanted to know, when her husband appeared there. "And, what is your name, again?" – this question addressed to her children. I was in some measure prepared, therefore, but not fully.

When Adeline would insist that she was not at Park Lane, I would attempt to reason with her and show her the park in front of the house. When figures appeared on the television screen in her bedroom and she would refuse to change in the presence of strange men, I would try to convince her that they were not really there, but images on a screen. It took me a long time to realize that this is not the approach one uses with persons suffering from senility and dementia. The important thing, I learned, is to ensure that physically and emotionally they are well cared for. The rest is really immaterial.

Things came to a head at the beginning of 1995. The weekend helper Judy had conveniently disappeared along with items of value and sentiment which my mother had usually kept sequestered in her wardrobe. Maybe we should have taken more seriously Adeline's earlier instruction that we remove Judy from Park Lane.

The real shocker came when we discovered that the housekeeper, Christine (a woman who had been in my mother's employ for several years, even before I had returned to Trinidad), had taken advantage of Adeline's trust in her, by getting her to sign blank bank debit slips and subsequently withdrawing sums of money from her account. By this time, and because of the deterioration of her mental state, Adeline would not have understood what had transpired and so had to be kept out of the picture. Worse, the culprit could not be confronted because this discovery was made on the eve of my departure on a 10-week consultancy which would take me as far away as Rome. We needed her to continue working at least until I returned home.

What a bitter pill that was to swallow! Luckily, my brother and I had in the interim followed up on our recognition that the move would have had to come sooner rather than later. We had done our research and contracted with a retirement home, the head of which was actually a former nurse and someone with whom Adeline had worked and had had, in earlier times, a friendship and good professional relationship. Presiding over such a move was not easy for me but my mother's safety and security were now clearly at risk and this had to assume priority.

Work Related Challenges Too!

The challenges had not been limited to my personal life, however. Two years into my tenure at CNIRD while at a meeting in Jamaica, I received the chilling news that the campus building housing my office had burned down and none of my files and other information had been saved. Luckily the news came at the end of the meeting and by the time I got home a plan had been formulated in my mind. The greatest challenge was to find new accommodation and within a couple of weeks this was secured in the St. Augustine area. But what about the files? It was the network that came to my rescue.

These were the days preceding widespread use of email and the internet generally. But fax machines were widely in use. I sent messages to each and every one of my colleagues, asking them to go through their own files and send me copies of everything relative to CNIRD. At the level of the management committee, my co-chairman, based at the St. Augustine campus, simply brought over all his files containing the entire history of the organization since I had made a point of sharing all relevant documentation with him. Teamwork and cooperation had come to the rescue once again.

We utilized this unfortunate event to our advantage as well, seeing it as time to become fully computerized and so we did. Moreover, because we were now renting our own space where no restrictions could be placed on us as had happened on the campus, we bought new furniture and arranged the office space in a way that was both utilitarian and attractive.

As if a fire were not enough, 1989 was the same year my plane crash-landed as it was taking off from Costa Rica where I had gone to attend a meeting. It was at that final point of takeoff when one normally hears the back wheels leave the tarmac, that there was a loud explosion and the plane fell violently back to the ground. Immediately all the oxygen masks presented themselves and some passengers started to scream. The plane was careening down the runway at breakneck speed. It finally came to a halt and this was followed by an announcement which indicated that passengers should immediately leave the aircraft via whichever exit was nearest to them.

I had no idea which was nearest to me and I remained strapped in my seat – Ms. Super Cool – while everyone else rushed around. Finally, I was approached by one of the frantic flight attendants who told me that I had to leave the plane. Now! And that I had to leave through the rear of the aircraft, all other options by then having been exhausted. I picked up my handbag and my shopping bag filled with the craft items I had purchased in the duty-free section of the airport and teetered uncertainly in my high heels toward the rear of the aircraft where the other flight attendants stood, all waiting for me, the final passenger, to leave the aircraft. But, unfortunately, this was not going to be such an easy function to discharge.

The fact of the matter is that, in all my years of travel, so many times aboard so many aircraft, I had never ever once picked up the "Safety on Board" instruction manual even to give it a passing glance. I therefore had no idea, not until I stood before the open exit of the downed aircraft, that I would be descending, not via steps but via a chute. A chute, moreover, which seemed to stretch forever downwards, without ever reaching the ground because the aircraft had crash landed on its other side. While the chute oscillated crazily in mid-air, about three men stood at the bottom, urging me on, telling me that they would catch me. (*Really!?*) Still wearing my high-heeled shoes and clutching my shopping and handbag even more tightly now, I sat down at the top of the exit chute very gingerly, oblivious of the now near hysteria of the cabin staff who, eventually, had to push me off. I froze, unable to move a muscle.

True to their word, the men at the bottom of the chute caught me in mid-air and deposited me gently on the ground, urging me to run! Run! Finally, reality struck and the shoes came off. I ran for all I was worth, barefoot and hyperventilating, across that tarmac, expecting the plane to explode at any second. When I finally made it into the terminal building and looked back to see what I had left behind, my mouth fell open in horror. The plane had collapsed entirely upon its side, the side away from which I had exited, and looked like a heap of distressed metal. I couldn't bear to watch. For two days, we were accommodated at a hotel in San José until repairs had been completed and the all-clear given to leave. That particular airline apparently had a history of mishaps and did not survive for much longer.

The Dream Plan Takes Up Residence in My Imagination

Throughout all of these various happenings and events, nonetheless, I had not forgotten nor given up on my retirement plan and

Visit to an indigenous market in Nairobi, Kenya

dream. It was a straightforward plan really. On the cocoa estate in Tobago where my father, Reginald, had toiled as he tried to fulfill his dream, I would establish an environmentally friendly retreat that would have three components: residential, agricultural and horticultural. The developmental principles with which I had become familiar over the years would be applied in the establishment of this project. Local material would be utilized for construction and furnishing and local labour would be employed in the construction and implementation phases. This would give the surrounding villages the opportunity to be the main beneficiaries of any economic impact or return. The cultivation of at least some of the food to be served to the clientele, the preparation of indigenous dishes, and adherence to environmental principles via the utilization of as many natural products as possible and composting as a means of waste disposal would all form part of the approaches to be employed. In addition, the buildings would be designed to make use of as much natural light and air as possible, eliminating or diminishing the need for power-generated appliances in this regard.

It was to be a green project run on rural development principles. This would be my way of not merely showing appreciation for all I had learned and been exposed to over the years since Geneva but would also demonstrate practically that these principles worked and could bring economic benefit to a rural entrepreneur. What helped is that the estate is situated on the edge of Tobago's rainforest and although the whole valley was once a series of cocoa estates, these unfortunately had all been devastated by Hurricane Flora in 1963, which gave the rainforest the opportunity to move in and take over, so to speak. A number of rivers and streams also meander across the valley and birds of several species have made the area their home.

Actually, the dawn chorus in the valley is positively overwhelming. It was perfect for my project which was designed to give persons the opportunity to immerse themselves in raw nature, appreciate the peace, simplicity and quiet of its natural charms and forget the noisiness of the world outside – a nature retreat in more ways than one. The agricultural and horticultural components of the project would be an important means of integrating development components into the project. How could one plan for a nature retreat without producing natural foods for consumption? How could one omit from the equation the introduction of flowering trees providing sustenance to encourage the propagation and development of wildlife?

I used every opportunity to discuss the plan with persons whose input I thought would be important. (Many did not think I was serious!) I looked at projects in other countries – Belize and Jamaica in particular – which I thought could provide some guidance. I researched the topic of environmental tourism. I had my friend Ancilla, who worked at the Caribbean Development Bank in Barbados, research their library and send me everything she could find on the cultivation of anthuriums and ginger lilies. I even looked into the possibilities of rehabilitating the remaining cocoa on the estate but the experts said the trees were too old for that purpose. I saved and I planned. I was getting there, but rather more slowly than I had hoped.

It was then that the realization struck me – my job, of necessity, was preoccupying most of my time, leaving insufficient opportunity to plan and implement my all-important project. I would have to leave CNIRD and focus on greater saving, planning and the commencement of my own project. After spending a full five years with the organization, I resigned in December 1992, leaving it rather more in the black than I had found it. The new director would have none of my problems.

It was January 1993 and I had a plan. I would spend the first two or three months of the year relaxing and reading some serious literature which I had not before found the time to do (Eric Williams' *Capitalism and Slavery* was, for example, on my list). I would write to my long established funding partners, letting them know that I was now in the market for any available consultancies and, most importantly, rest and reflect. The idea was that with the consultancies, not only would I be able to earn more and therefore save more, but I would be better able to control my time, thus leaving me the requisite opportunities for pursuing my long-term project.

I thought this was an excellent plan until one of my friends, an accountant by profession, said to me casually one day, "So, I suppose you have a number of consultancy projects lined up?" "Well, actually no," I confessed sheepishly, the wonderful plan immediately starting to assume shades of a fool's paradise. "I plan to write to people I know and I assumed they would have work for me...." Not a word did she respond, but the skepticism on her face was enough to galvanize me into action, however. Deciding against the long-awaited break, I immediately began sending off those letters. Within a month I was already at work, which effectively and definitively put paid to my plans for relaxation and reading.

The consultancies, however, opened up a whole new phase of interesting work for me as well as allowed me to utilize my knowledge and experience in the field of rural development. Many of these assignments were evaluations of projects and programmes that had been in existence over three- to five-year periods and all were based in the Caribbean. This made it relatively easy for me to understand the issues of the project holders as well as, based on what had been successful elsewhere in the region, to recommend solutions to problems identified. The networking experience of CNIRD was proving to be invaluable, even to some of those agencies which had viewed it with hostility at the beginning. Ultimately, the experiences I encountered as a consultant would also prove to be extremely useful to me as an entrepreneur with no backing from funding agencies or a management committee!

Enter Husband #2

It was about this time too that I met the man who was to become my second husband. I like to think that we met "by microwave", as I enjoyed describing it. There was a decided history to this event.

After leaving Adeline's house, I moved into the townhouse I had purchased, only to find that the kitchen was so small that it could not contain a full-sized stove with an oven. What was I going to do? At least some of my food had to be baked! I discussed this with the townhouse agent and he suggested that a microwave oven might be the answer. A microwave oven? What was this? Surprised at my ignorance (this was 1985) but patient all the same, he explained that it was an appliance small enough to fit on my counter top and do the job of baking with which I was concerned.

I had never really interested myself in expensive devices but instead merely aimed to acquire whatever basic item was required to fulfill my needs comfortably. Moreover, my assignments in Grenada had ensured that there would be no time for knowledge of such gadgetry, far less acquisition of these contrivances. Finally, having returned to live in Trinidad at my mother's house, one could be assured that everything was as intact as it had been for several years. A new item on the market such as this would surely not have come to her attention or generated any interest!

Well, a microwave oven now seemed to be just the answer since I had the counter space to accommodate it and so the appliance was duly purchased. In the end, so greatly did I enjoy its use that I wondered how I had existed for all those years without one. In fact, even after I had moved out of the townhouse and into an independent house with a full-sized kitchen, I continued to depend on the use of my microwave oven. Until catastrophe struck.... Clearly, I was still a novice in the school of detachment.

Working in St. Augustine had afforded me the privilege to go home to Tacarigua for lunch and this I would do once I could. I would cook lunch for the children and myself in the morning and at lunchtime would use the microwave to reheat mine. I don't think I ever once heated a meal in the microwave without remembering what used to happen before my introduction to this appliance. The meal would have to be placed in a pot of water, covered, and left to simmer for a possible fifteen minutes before it could be ready to be eaten. Moreover, one needed to be careful of the utensil used since plastic would melt and ware could break. A microwave oven allowed the use of both plastic and ware and a meal ready to be eaten in two or three minutes. Here certainly were the ingredients to allow a busy working mother to become addicted to a mechanism which made life so entirely easy. Did I also mention that it could roast a leg of lamb or pork to a turn? And that it had an element which facilitated browning?

Catastrophically, one day, as I attempted to lift the lever handle to open the microwave and claim my lunch, it mysteriously broke off in my hand, leaving the door locked. Frankly, at that moment I didn't know which situation was worse – non-access to my lunch (I do not usually have breakfast) or non-access to the microwave. Lunch had to be first! I phoned up a friend who suggested the use of a screw driver, using the flat tip to prise open the door of the oven, which I did, thus securing access to my lunch. For the next few days I became skilled in the art of opening and closing it this way but was somewhat uncomfortable with this procedure. I decided to approach the company where I had bought the appliance to purchase a new handle. I called and was referred to the service manager who told me that sadly, they were all out of stock of that item. I then ordered the part directly from the manufacturer and it arrived about three weeks later.

At the time, I was having some cupboards installed and had arranged with the joiner, a jack of all trades, that he would replace the handle of the microwave. In the end, this was not possible since we discovered that only a portion of the handle had been sent, putting me back to square one. I approached the local company for a second time. The Service Manager had some good news for me this time. They now had the part in stock. Indeed, there was just one left and it would be held for me. I dropped by and collected it as soon as I could. Given that the joiner had completed his job with me and moved on to other projects, we had agreed that I would call him as soon as I obtained the new part. This is when the fun really started.

It would appear that in the midst of writing his telephone number something had distracted me and I never took down the last four digits. No problem, I thought. I would contact the person who had put me on to him in the first place. I did, but only to discover that she did not have a number for him either.

There was only one thing to do – phone the service manager and ask him whether his company could send someone to do the necessary installation. Having heard where I lived, he offered to come by himself, since he had to pass there on his way home. I must say it did not happen right away and I had to call with about three reminders before he finally arrived in February of 1991 and fixed the handle of my microwave.

We chatted idly during that first visit but what struck me was that the day happened to be Valentine's Day and he had brought along flowers. He said that the flowers were for me but, frankly, I was unwilling to accept them, skeptical that they might really have been meant for someone else. (I didn't know this man!) He persuaded me that they weren't, however, and somewhat reluctantly, if graciously, I accepted the flowers. After a couple of weeks, he called and suggested a visit to which I was amenable since I had enjoyed his company the first time. Thereafter a pattern of regular social calls ensued. This guy was cool, laid back, acceptable to my daughter who liked him and we shared, it seemed, the same basic philosophies and approaches to life.

It would be inaccurate to say that Chez (as I shall refer to him) and I dated. Rather, he visited several times per week on his way home from work and on some weekends, we went on long country drives which we both enjoyed. It was an easy, laid-back relationship without stress or drama. Several months later he asked what I wanted for a birthday present and, when I demurred, suggested that that present be an engagement ring. There was surprise but little hesitation on my part in accepting. I had taken him into my confidence some months earlier, telling him about my dream project in Tobago and so it was agreed that we would celebrate the engagement by travelling to Tobago (he had never been there before) so that he could have a first-hand look at what I was planning to do.

In the meantime, my family was not exactly rip-roaringly enthusiastic about my plan to develop this project. As far as Adeline was concerned, this was a backward rather than a forward move, after all the effort she had invested in my education. Here I was, moving from Trinidad to rural Tobago! My brother abandoned his usual *sang-froid* to advise, with a look of deep concern on his features, that he did not think that Cuffie River, given its location, was "a safe place for a single woman to live" (this was before Chez came on the scene). Even Marina, my sister, normally supportive of all I did, asked me whether I was sure that this is what I wanted to do. Of course, I was sure and nothing was going to deter me. Moreover, there was now someone in my life, a strong male presence, who looked like he might be willing and able to help in the fulfillment of this dream!

Having visited Tobago and the project site and initially suggesting that maybe I could engage in some other activity (*Good Lord, you too?!*) Chez finally comprehended my determination and passion and offered to participate in my plans. In fact, I was completely taken aback to learn from him that he was not simply the technician I knew him to be, but was also sufficiently acquainted with building construction to allow for the organization and supervision of my long-planned project. (*Really?*) He convinced me that I did not need my Tobago contractor, Mr. McDonald, after all. I admit that I did wonder whether I was perhaps being somewhat foolhardy in simply accepting the word of someone who, let's be honest, I had not known for any extended period and whose skills in the construction arena could well have been more imaginary than real! Nonetheless, I took the information as a very good omen, released my proposed contractor and got down to the job of seriously planning the start of the project.

The Retreat Project Is Launched

At the start of 1993, I took the first big steps toward achieving the establishment of my Tobago eco-retreat on the same estate on which my father Reginald had lived and from where he had commuted to Chaguanas to spend time with his wife and children. I used this and the following year well in respect of advancing my project plans. I purchased house design and home décor magazines at the various metropolitan airports through which I travelled and pored over them in transit to see what fresh and innovative ideas I could garner. I looked with a critical eye at my various hotel rooms to determine what I liked, what I didn't and what was missing – all with a view to helping me decide on the final look and feel which my place would have. Thus, I measured, I drew sketches, I took photographs or simply wrote descriptive paragraphs about what I liked. I was busy! In the end, I had whole folders of designs, articles, ideas and sketches. In principle, I knew that I wanted a building which would be designed to make the greatest use of natural air and natural light. As many natural materials as possible – such as clay, wood, bamboo, stone, etc. – would go into its construction and everything would be purchased locally. Workers would be hired from the surrounding villages. Chez and I got married later that year and he was fully on board with the planning.

Given that this period also took me to Caribbean islands and other places I had never before visited – the British Virgin Islands, the Turks and Caicos Islands, Montserrat, Anguilla, Barbuda, and Nevis – I had the opportunity to acquire both general and particular information which would add to my storehouse of knowledge regarding the actual management of my future enterprise once it was up and running. I remember, for example, while staying at a very large hotel in Georgetown, Guyana being impressed by the fact that, despite the many guests staying there, the staff always addressed me by name. It made me feel that I was important to them and I noted this as one aspect which I would adopt when the time came to run my own business.

And Then Came 1995: A Year to Remember!

In 1995, I turned 50. As I do at the start of each new decade, I had put my plans in place, plans which did not envisage the announcement by my son that I was going to become a grandmother for the first time. *Be Prepared!* My girl guide motto screamed at me, but to no avail. Was I ready? Was I not too "young"? What was going to be expected of me in this capacity? In the end, it was the practice of detachment which helped me to take it all in stride and to soldier on. After all, my permission was not needed nor was I being asked to participate in any way in raising this child.

My daughter, Lara, had an announcement of her own, thankfully less surprising and easier for me to wrap my head around – she had been accepted by the Boston University School of Management and would be commencing her studies later that year. Frank, now living in Boston himself and with a professorship at Boston College (clearly, he had fulfilled *his* lifelong dream!) would be on hand to give her the support she would need – moral and otherwise. With both my children having now achieved adult status, it left me free to focus my undivided attention on my third and possibly most challenging "newborn" – the establishment and development of the Cuffie River Nature Retreat. Construction work on the project began in earnest, after ten years of dreaming, saving, envisioning and projecting.

Chez took up residence in Tobago in January of 1995, hired workers, ordered material and formally began construction of my long-planned project. He was the man on the ground, in charge of the works; I was the fundraiser, accountant and interior designer. I had thought it not unreasonable to expect that in a couple of years everything would be completed and so began to do the marketing of the project. I also began the winding down of the consultancy work I had begun in 1993, generally preparing myself for life in Tobago and the launch of the Cuffie River Nature Retreat. Things did not go as smoothly as planned, however. Completion was much further away than I had ever envisaged and the challenges being encountered were more than I could ever have believed possible. And so, it would be back to the consultancy drawing board to earn more money to finance the construction. There were approaches to banks and lending institutions, drawing up of project development plans and proposals – now subjectively, for myself and not objectively for project holders in the field – and planning and budgeting at every turn.

First, there was the access road to the project, a road which was really a cart trace and had seen no improvement since the days when my father had used it. Amazingly, it was still maintained by the government Infrastructure and Road Works Division on a fairly regular basis, despite the fact that no one lived along the road except those right at its entrance. Here was a road, clearly not meant for vehicular traffic, parts of which turned to mud from the slightest rainfall and which, even with a four-wheel drive vehicle, made for precipitous driving. At the very end of this road one encountered a river, across which there was no bridge! To gain access to the property meant crossing this river on foot. Nightmares immediately presented themselves. How were the steel and the lumber, not to mention bags of cement, to get to the project site? Surely a bridge was the first order of the day.

Accordingly, I arranged a meeting with the relevant political authority who advised me to write a letter of request for the construction of a bridge to facilitate access to agricultural lands and have it signed by as many persons as possible who owned lands in the vicinity. This I did. Approval was granted and by March of that year the bridge-building project was underway. The truck drivers nevertheless were reluctant to use our local road and in the end, only one solitary driver could be persuaded to do so. He was our saviour, but the experience one night of having to run around looking for a backhoe to pull his heavily laden truck from the mud in which it had become stuck remains in my memory.

There was next the question of having actual access to the materials needed for building. Acquiring materials of a client's choice with ease and facility and having them transported to a building site was not a undertaking which one could take for granted in Tobago in 1995 as one could in Trinidad. In many cases, in fact, the materials were not even available in Tobago. If one could not wait while the hardware store in turn waited for them to be sent from Trinidad, it would require journeying to Trinidad and fetching them oneself. Luckily, Chez had his own 3-ton Mazda truck and many were the trips made to and from Trinidad for purchases of this nature.

Transport was via the ferry service operating between Trinidad and Tobago and in 1995 there was no fast ferry service, as there is now. The journey would therefore take at least five hours between the islands, barring a breakdown which happened all too frequently. Arriving with a truckload of stuff, one did not immediately exit the ferry and so usually Chez did not arrive home until about 11 p.m. Next morning, ferry lag or not, everyone was expected to hit the ground running, hoping that there would be no rain. Nonetheless, with Trinidad and Tobago the beneficiary of a dry and a wet season, hope did not get one very far on entering the month of June. Though the official rainy season would run its course from June to November/December, work was expected to continue anyway.

Rural development principles require, among other things, that projects which are developed in any given community give first priority to the people of that community. Thus it was that the labour force for the project in both the construction and the operational stages was expected to be drawn from the nearby villages. The problem was that the vast majority of persons were unskilled and therefore had to be taught on the job. This was no easy task and I recall a whole floor from which tiles had to be removed because they had been placed helter-skelter by a worker who did not have the requisite skill to do the job properly. The other challenge was the brick-laying. We were using smooth-faced bricks to give a natural finish to the exterior. Unlike regular bricks which are plastered after they are laid, these bricks are intended to lie bare to the world and thus have to be laid very neatly. What a challenge this turned out to be for labour *and* management!

Utilities were another problematic issue. Two and a half miles down a road on which no one lives hardly creates the expectation of there being electricity or running water at the end and, so said, there was neither to be had. Luckily the nearby river provided a good source of fresh, clean water for drinking as well as for mixing concrete and other tasks associated with the construction. The provision of electricity, however, did not present so easy a solution. Whereas in a context in which its presence would allow for some extra work to be done at the end of a day or an additional shift to come on board after sundown, there could be no such option in this case. Unadulterated darkness prevailed from as early as 5.30 p.m. There was also the question of utilizing power tools to produce results at a faster and much easier pace. Instead, hand tools had to be laboriously employed to get the various tasks done and when it became absolutely necessary to have a power supply, a portable generator was rented.

But by far the most irksome problem to be resolved was obtaining government permission to undertake a project of this nature. Despite what I had worked so hard at saving, additional funds soon became necessary for the completion of the eco-retreat. One of the major challenges in acquiring these funds was that funding consideration was contingent on the granting of permission by the relevant government authority for its construction. I was now experiencing in real time the frustrations of my former project holders when they were forced to interact with the bureaucracy! What I was to discover is that all of Tobago, with the exception of Scarborough, is zoned for agriculture and the project was located very definitively outside of Scarborough – in a rural area.

The authorities, true to form, refused to grant planning permission on the ground that this was not an agricultural project. Time and again, I made the case that the project had an agricultural component, that it was going to be providing employment for a rural community, that the agricultural lands were lying idle anyway, with the youth showing no interest in that area of economic development. But all to no avail. The functionaries were adamant, that is, until a senior officer stepped into the picture, saw the logic of what I had been presenting and what I was aiming to do. Finally, the building plan was approved in July 1997!

My ability to write project proposals of an economic nature would now come to the fore and although the project as presented would be endorsed by the project officers who in fact commended it, there would be a waiting period of a further six months before approval was actually granted. Other professionals from the organization (architects, engineers, etc.) had to visit, analyse and give their approval, followed by another seven months before the building was sufficiently complete to open its doors to the public in August of 1998.

Frustrating as they were, these were not the only challenges to emerge in 1995, however. One morning in March I was awakened at 6 a.m. by my neighbour who wanted to know why was my garage gate standing wide open and my car gone from said garage. Stupefied I checked, only to find that she was correct. The police, when contacted, assured me that they would do their best but recommended that I also do my own investigation, which I did. Well, it seems that neither investigation turned up anything since not even a trace of the vehicle was ever found.

I convinced myself, in the spirit of detachment taught me by my Raja Yoga, that the car was only something material, that my health and safety were much more important and that no one had attempted to harm me in the process of stealing the vehicle. Further, given the great deal of travelling that year outside of Trinidad, I would hardly miss the vehicle. But I did wonder what role, if any, my dog had played – that now fully grown canine. Twice saved from abductors, now so huge that when he stood on his hind legs he was taller than the front gate and frightened everyone in the neighbourhood, except, it seemed, those who had stolen my vehicle.

After several months, I managed to secure another vehicle. I also installed an external alarm system designed to alert me should anyone enter the garage area. At two a.m. one morning, just one month after I had acquired the second vehicle, the alarm went off. At first, I thought it was the dog which had triggered the alarm and so bravely sauntered out to the garage area, drawing back the drapes from the sliding door which separated my home office from the garage. There, sitting complacently as if entering someone's property for the purpose of theft were the most natural thing in the world, was a young man who appeared to be waiting for the alarm to stop going off before he performed the illicit function which had brought him to my house. Without thinking that my personal safety might be at stake, I rapped sharply on the glass behind him. Shocked, he spun around and, in one fluid motion, leapt cleanly over my gate of not insubstantial height, followed by another whom I had not seen but who was obviously an accomplice.

I should have realized from that experience that I was a marked woman in respect of vehicle theft and should have left the vehicle elsewhere when travelling. But I didn't; and it was a mere two weeks later, while in St. Lucia, that I received a call that the thieves had returned – this time, successfully achieving their goal. All in 1995. Like the first vehicle, no sign of this vehicle would ever materialize.

Reflections on the (Bumpy) Road to Success

In a curious kind of way, life in Trinidad – this place to which I had been reluctant to return – had opened up several opportunities at the community-based and volunteer levels, and taken the life and professional skills I had acquired over the years several notches higher. It was as if the time had arrived for all of the strands of earlier happenings to be woven together into some kind of cohesive whole. Thus, it was that while I lived in Trinidad I sat on the executive of the parent teacher association of one of my children's schools. Also, starting as a mere member of the country's Blind Welfare Association, I was ultimately elected as its president and served for two terms. In addition, I chaired one of the standing committees of the credit union to which I belonged; was appointed a board member of a state institution; was a founding member and held an executive position in the residents' association started in my community; and was a founding member of a women's organization that continues to be active today.

Many of these positions were held simultaneously and, except for the position on the state board of directors, were all voluntary. In addition, there was my quite demanding job as head of a regional organization with both staff and programmes to supervise and, most importantly, the parenting of my children and, in many respects, of my mother. In reviewing all of this as I prepared to leave Trinidad and assume a position in Tobago so vastly different from anything I had ever done before, it occurred to me that there had indeed been valuable lessons learned which I could share.

I realized, for example, that for an organization to be effective it did not need to comprise masses of people. Small units, appropriately staffed, often allow for more effective action and results than might otherwise occur, one of the end results being the growth of the individuals who staff them. The CNIRD is a case in point. For the five-year period that I administered this organization, we never had a staff component greater than five, comprising both administrative and programme staff. Arlene and Melina, both wonderfully effective women, became so adept at taking charge of the administration, accounting and documentation aspects, that it left me all the time I needed to focus on programming and on fund-raising, with the assistance of a programme officer whose portfolio was regional in scope. CNIRD's management committee, all volunteers and each with a specific skill base, helped me to carve out and implement the policy approaches we needed. We worked consistently and collaboratively and our results were always positive.

Teamwork really was the key to our success and is a lesson that should be replicated in any institution, whether community-based, public or private sector. It really does work! Teamwork implies communication and collaboration, a form of networking, and is possible in any context. This is one of the lessons I took with me into my private endeavour and it has proven its value in successful results over and over again. Whether at the personal or at the professional level, so much more is achieved and so much more easily when there is open communication.

It therefore made a great deal of sense for us at CNIRD to have regular meetings where persons could share their views. Decisions, when taken, would not appear to be those of the persons supposedly wielding some measure of power but of the majority, if not of all involved. Individuals who are made to feel that they are members of a team, that their opinions have been heard and sometimes adopted, even in modified fashion, who understand and feel ownership for the perspectives and the plans, are more likely to exercise such ownership by putting greater effort into the implementation of the tasks at hand.

Commitment to the process in which one is engaged is yet another relationship principle. With commitment comes the discipline needed to get the job done. So often procrastination steals away the energy required to succeed and by the time the various components are achieved, if at all, the potential impact has been lost. When one is committed to a process, to the development of a relationship, to the success of an endeavour, little or nothing stands in the way of goals, these goals having been clearly understood from the start. Linked to commitment is cooperation, given that hardly any project worthy of note can be accomplished by one person. Rather, it is the networking and team effort, cemented by commitment by all parties involved, which result in success and achievement.

How was I to utilize this mosaic of experiences in a way which would add value to this new and uncharted course I was about to undertake? Tobago, while not entirely foreign to me, was certainly not entirely familiar either. I was fairly confident about the ease with which I would settle in, but it was a confidence born of courage rather than based on fact. Then there was the question of operating, for the first time in my life, an enterprise which needed to be marketed for the purpose of generating profit. *Profit!* The very word was alien to me, who had worked for most of my adult life with non-profit organizations. Moreover, I had always thought of my enterprise as a project, one simply designed to demonstrate that a rural enterprise could be successful if managed along basic development principles. This was the challenge I had set myself and it was no good pretending that those close to me understood precisely where I was coming from. They did not. I think most people thought I was a bit crazy to be embarking on such a project, one which, as far as they were concerned, offered no clear guarantees of success.

Once more I was on my own here, it seemed.

I made my final move to Tobago in September of 1997. I hoped then and still do now that this would be the ultimate move in my rather chequered life existence. This was now the sixth major move from one land mass to another and, counting internal moves within countries, this made the total twelve. Twelve moves, six of them major. Some people spend all their lives in the spot where they were born. I, on the other hand, have criss-crossed this region and, in one instance moved from the Caribbean and across the Atlantic to Europe.

8 ✒ Tobago 1997 to the Present

The Building of the Dream

NOT LONG AGO I came across a pamphlet written in 1683 by Captain John Poyntz and entitled "The Present Prospect of the Famous and Fertile Island of Tobago". He described Tobago as he saw it:

> ...Thou art here presented with The Present Prospect of the Island of Tobago, about forty Leagues distant from Barbadoes; but far excelling that Island, and indeed any other of the Caribbe-Islands, in the Fertility and Richness of the Soil, and in the Commodiousness of its Bays and Harbour: And it is no Paradox to affirm That although it lies more South, the Air is as Cool and Refreshing as that of Barbadoes: and yet Exempted from those affrighting and destructive Hurricanes that have been often Fatal to the rest of the Caribbe-Islands...

True to what was expressed in the above piece, Tobago enjoys a richness of soil which allows almost anything to grow here, from cash crops to tree crops, from sugar cane to tobacco to cocoa. Such a beautiful island it is too. By any standards Tobago is small, but so diverse that in this single tiny area of 116 square miles, exist peaceful white sand beaches, reefs for snorkelling, diving possibilities, wildlife and bird-watching opportunities, wetlands, protected rainforest, turtle watching – you name it. Mountains, valleys, rivers and waterfalls are all in abundance. Motoring through the countryside is problematic as one must keep an eye on those winding roads and not admire the picturesque beauty of the villages and the natural landscape. There is an impression here of a sensitivity to preserving the natural environment for generations to come.

Rugged in topography, except for the strip which runs between Crown Point and Scarborough in the southwest, physically Tobago is like a smaller version of the lush "nature isle" of Dominica. In 1997, when I began to live here full-time, I could regularly view and admire the unspoiled and uncluttered landscape and could not help comparing the large tracts of open green spaces flaunting flora and fauna with the almost entirely built landscape which Trinidad has become. In Tobago, one does not have to travel to the rural areas to witness such scenes of environmental preservation. They are everywhere.

Located in a valley as I am, the wonder and joy are particularly fulfilling. From December to March both the immortelle with its flame-coloured flowers and the cypress with its large bunches of white blossoms are in bloom, the juxtaposition of which is enough to take one's breath away. In addition to all this are the sounds that greet one continuously on the property – the whistling of birds, the chirping of cicadas, the call of mating frogs, the rippling of the rivers which run on either side of the property, the rushing sound of the nearby waterfall. Tobago, far from being anything akin to a reflection of Trinidad, now presented itself to me as an island as different from Trinidad in its cultural norms and approaches as it is in size.

The first thing that struck me about Moriah, the village I now called home, was the fact that, in comparison to other rural communities I had encountered throughout the Caribbean, this one was very well endowed with facilities not normally seen in rural villages. I believe the villagers took this situation for granted. Here was a rural community of less than 2,000 persons, large by Tobago standards maybe, but small in absolute terms, and boasting several amenities. In 1997, when I began to live here, there were two primary schools, an early childhood learning centre, a post office *and* a postal agency, a police station, a community centre, a health centre, an agricultural station, a credit union and, of course, churches (at least five) of varying denominations. It was a rural development activist's dream.

Yet where are the groups, I asked the residents, of farmers, of women, of youth, of the general community? Each time I enquired, I was pointed in the direction of the Village Council. But citizens of Trinidad and Tobago know that village councils comprise community groupings which tend to be politically associated. Of the other people-based, nonpolitical voluntary groups, there was no sign. Struck by an idea, I decided to attempt to facilitate the formation of a volunteer community group. But how was one to start? I knew no one in the community but I did have rural community development experience which directed me to find the information I needed. On the basis of asking around, certain questions addressed to selected persons, I readily identified a young man, Sheldon, whom I approached and asked if he would meet with me.

What was encouraging about finding Sheldon, this community activist, was the fact that he was a youngster – just about 20 years old. With his help, a Village Improvement Committee was established, a group comprising male and female residents, professionals and tradesmen, young and not so young. We met regularly, planned, implemented, fundraised. Projects such as the vacation camp held in the month of August were well sponsored and well supported by the community. In turn, we identified activities which we thought would be of interest or assistance to the community at large. Unfortunately, the demise of this organization followed the same pattern as that of so many others – once the main personality spearheading the momentum withdraws, wholly or partially, a similar motion follows within the organization itself.

I had come to Tobago to establish an enterprise which now finally appeared ready to receive my complete attention and so was unable to put all my effort into the community organization as I had previously. Try as I might, the issue of succession just never caught hold within the membership and sadly, I watched as this committee, which promised so much, ended up with a track record, perhaps, but insufficient longevity to make the required dent in the community.

Life, particularly in Tobago's rural areas, is simple, healthy and pure. Here in the bush, as it were, I felt an authenticity, a rejuvenation, a better understanding of myself and of the natural environment surrounding me. Rural communities in Tobago display on an everyday basis the tenets of what is accepted as good rural development planning and implementation: domestic rearing of livestock and poultry; a typical kitchen garden; fruit trees in the backyard, in many instances planted decades ago by ancestors. The net result of all of this is that the standard of living and quality of life in Tobago are generally higher than in Trinidad – this, despite the fact that not only is Trinidad more developed, so to speak, than Tobago, but the cost of living is higher here.

Living in Tobago, I discovered that the murmurings and complaints which had been emanating from Tobago for more years than I can remember were more than justified. It struck me particularly when construction began and the problems described earlier were encountered. Things became worse when legal and official issues had to be dealt with. Big sister Trinidad held all the cards and called all the shots. I had always been sympathetic to the plight of Tobagonians because all my mother's close relatives were from here. But, it is only when one actually resides in Tobago that the full extent of the bias makes its mark. While I must make note of the fact that things have improved significantly in this regard over the period that I have lived here, there is still room for further progress.

I remember the officer at the Town and Country Planning Division who, just before she denied my application for building approval for the second time, asked me whether I thought Tobago was in a worse off position than, say, Toco in Trinidad. "Absolutely," I replied – and then continued:

> At least the person from Toco, at the end of a fruitless day, can return home, sleep in her own bed, and make the trip once more into Port of Spain the following morning. Frustrating and inconvenient, perhaps, but far better than the person from Tobago. She, in turn, would have to put things in place in order to be away for at least 24 hours, and journey overnight [there being no fast ferry at the time] to get to Trinidad in time to meet the officers the following day. Disappointed in this regard, however, she must find some-where to spend yet a second night in Trinidad, change her ferry ticket, if this is possible, all the while not knowing whether one's mission will be successful.

Of course, she never replied, but clearly my argument held no weight for her since my application was denied a second time.

So here I was, in this place I had dreamed of and in which I had planned to reside, to conduct a business of which I knew hardly anything but utilizing principles with which I was very familiar. Bit by bit, I was slowly settling into my new abode. All the staff were recruited from the village and I learned a great deal from them by way of information sometimes casually shared. I learned, for example, that my village has a very high percentage of twins, that genetically, many families have had twins appearing along the lines of their genealogy. In fact, one evening, between two of the women, they counted twenty sets of twins, spanning about three genera-tions that they knew in the village – a village of barely two thousand people.

From Vision to Reality

In August of 1998 the Cuffie River Nature Retreat opened its doors to the public. My joy was immense. Notably, I experienced the sense that for the first time I was co-existing with both my parents – my mother who had guided me through most of my life by word and example and now also my father, whom I never knew but whose spirit I began to be acutely aware of. This is when I began to understand what must have motivated my father to believe that, without the benefit of descent from a family of landowners and agricultural entrepreneurs, he could purchase and operate a cocoa estate. It explained too, his opting for a frugal lifestyle of food, water, shelter – while he made efforts to get his project off the ground. When I looked at the old cocoa trees, I saw his back-breaking effort. When I heard the small waterfall, which gushes into the river which runs below the Retreat, I imagined him relaxing in its shallow waters at the end of a long day of work. When I looked up at the hill overlooking the Retreat I saw in my mind's eye the little hut in which he lived. It was as if both my parents had now joined forces to watch over me and ensure that the project would succeed.

Mine had been the task of getting down to the serious business of completing the project and making it viable, demonstrating that a rural enterprise, despite what appeared to be the odds, really could work along sound principles of development. I think the most important lesson I continued to apply was that of teamwork, the nurturing and maintaining of relationships given that I was now embarking on a type of exercise which in very many ways was completely alien to anything I had ever done before. For starters, mine was the sole responsibility for hiring and training yet interacting with the workers as a member of one team. In retrospect, I think this has been the greatest challenge of all. I had to put aside some of the habits and principles which I had developed over the years as well as others which came naturally to me, virtually undergoing certain personality changes in the process. The rewards have been positive, however.

For several years and up to the time of writing this memoir, the enterprise has boasted of a small but gifted team of workers who, I believe, are contented – if one is to judge by the length of time they have remained in the employ of the Retreat. Besides, they are reliable, efficient, hard-working and pleasant to the guests who are always high in their praise of them. It took me little time to realize that the well-being of the workers takes priority over that of the guests for the simple reason that, once you get the former right, the latter tends to automatically take care of itself. Here again, a basic principle of rural development has saved the day – the issue of putting people first, of focusing on their welfare and ensuring that everything possible is done to continuously achieve that goal or set of goals. This, to my mind, is the essence of true and committed leadership. If only our politicians could understand this....

The learning process was evident at other levels as well. I had had absolutely no knowledge or experience at organizing or running any type of hospitality facility, and wondered where to start. I decided then that given my track record of organizing and running a household, I could do it, once I treated the Retreat as a household project but on a larger scale. The issue of food was another, even more challenging one. I had been used to small families and therefore small amounts of cooking. How did one even begin to plan for cooking for large numbers? I decided to err on the side of caution and, throwing discretion (and money, I suppose) to the wind, merely served up three large meals daily to ensure that the guests felt they were getting their money's worth.

There was much groaning about the amount of food served but they ate it all anyway, until finally, a tour operator from Germany set me straight. He advised me that people from cold climates really do have a preference for consuming lighter meals in the middle of the day with the larger meals in the evening. "It's just so hot in the middle of the day and having to digest the heavy meal makes us sluggish," he said. Another regular visitor, John, who ended up being a firm friend and now acts as my representative for the United Kingdom and the wider Europe, further convinced me to lighten the portions served: "They will eat it because you are serving it to them," he argued. "But it is simply too much and you are wasting money." Finally convinced after he had been reciting this mantra for well over a year (he came twice yearly), I followed his advice and found it to be correct.

Many were the good ideas I received from persons who heard about the Retreat and decided to drop by to have a look, some of them with hotel management experience which I did not have. Moreover, the actual users of the rooms, the guests, were always asked to give their candid comments and suggestions. Between these two sources of information, helpful data was gathered and ideas put into effect. Some took several years to implement; others could be done almost right away.

Take the issue of the swimming pool, for example. I had made a conscious and deliberate decision that there would be no pool since the use of chlorine went against all my principles about operating a nature retreat. How could one be true to those principles and create a situation which would have a negative impact on people's skin and hair? But time after time, in the suggestions solicited from the guests, the idea of having a pool would be raised as a means of relaxation after a long walk in the woods; for the benefit of children who might have accompanied their parents; for spouses who would rather lounge in or by the pool than walk in the woods. I began to raise the issue openly with the guests and one day was rewarded by one who told me that I did not have to use chlorine at all since there now existed *salt* pools. She had one herself, she said. So, dutifully, I looked it up on the Internet and began my search. Today, and for the past several years, the pool, elevated in design to avoid putting a large hole in the ground, is one of the major highlights of the Retreat, competing with the birds and the food for high praise. It was the issue of communication that saved the day here.

Meanwhile, the business was limping along, not by any means reaching the point of take-off that a business requires but nonetheless earning income. Why wasn't I worried? The truth is that I was driven by two main considerations. The first was that, in succeeding my father on land where he had established but was unable to achieve his dream project because of his early demise, I was, in a sense, continuing the realization of that dream, albeit somewhat differently. The second consideration was that the establishment of this project allowed me to unequivocally and totally demonstrate that rural development principles when properly applied, do result in outcomes of success. The ability to pay my staff and my mortgage was far more important to me than turning a profit in the project's early stages. Instead, the comfort of the guests, the service we provided, contented staff – all these were what, in my view, determined its success based on the fundamentals in which I had learned to believe and to respect over the years. Nonetheless, I worked very hard at marketing it, following up every lead suggested to me as useful. The value of networking and communication!

This Question of Relationships!

Meanwhile, Chez had been busy. Based on the success of constructing the beautiful edifice that Cuffie River Nature Retreat turned out to be, job offers were emerging for him. In a sense, this was the start of the changes which began to erode the relationship. Relationships! Hadn't I reflected long and hard on these before coming to Tobago? But as human beings, we are prone to change. Or, simply, we fail to see the cumulative impact of isolated issues which might be irritating to our partners. If we see them as mainly discrete points in question, then often no lessons are learned and behavioural patterns do not change. From being so supportive of each other, planning together, doing things together, our joint lives had now moved into two separate strands of existence.

In a sense, perhaps this was natural. People after all do change and, for us both, there had been life-changing occurrences and experiences, exposure to events which can sometimes result in the virtual end of an era. In an effort to make the union successful, I had tried to virtually reinvent myself, to be and to do what I had never before been and done – a helpmate who demurred fully to her husband's wishes, who challenged nothing and accepted everything. But not only was this so out of character for me that I ended up being miserable, it changed nothing in terms of reaction from the very party on whose behalf it was undertaken. It was as if this was supposed to be the norm, the expectation, with no mutual response forthcoming.

So, reminiscent of Adeline in the mid-1930s when she joined Reginald in New York only to find that her life there was miserable given that she was now not only dependent on her spouse but also unable to practice her beloved nursing, Regina now took her life back. Relationships are great when the principles guiding them are mutually established and respected since, as the old folks say, *one hand cyar clap* and I seemed to be twisting myself into contortions to clap with one hand. What would work for me? I asked myself. What suits *me* and would ensure my happiness? Certainly not fighting and struggling to mould a relationship which had now transmuted into one quite unlike its original shape and form. I had never been encouraged by my mother to just settle but rather to push myself to achieve worthwhile goals.

I found myself taking a hard look at other couples, especially those who had been living together for over twenty years. How many of them, women in particular, are really happy, I asked myself? How many, for the sake of appearances, the sake of the children, security, religion, perhaps experiencing some sense of humiliation or shortcoming, will endure a relationship which is not fulfilling? How many have suffered the heartache caused by a partner's infidelity? For, let's not fool ourselves, with all the relaxation of ideas that has taken place in society, the cards continue to be stacked in favour of men. Our communities (women included), continue to be more generous and forgiving of our menfolk than of women.

When I pose these questions to my women friends, they respond by saying, "Not everyone is like you, Regina." They tell me that not every woman has the courage and the discipline it takes to hold her own and continuously apply the principles which she might have established for herself. Maybe they are right. But sometimes I think it is good old-fashioned pride and the strength taught me by Adeline that keeps me on the straight and narrow – that pride that says I must work with the hand I have dealt myself and have the strength to face the consequences of my decisions. No one is holding a gun to my head, after all. But, isn't that what it always comes down to, a person's right to choose, to choose the path he or she must take and live with it? Some are contented with situations which are far from perfect but accept to live with them nonetheless. A few others, like me, want to go past that state. We want to be perfectly happy and fulfilled; we want to honour the commitments we have made to ourselves, entirely.

The good news is that, in my critical examination of couples, I have found a few who really seem to have nailed it down. They seem genuinely suited to each other and appear to be really happy together and respectful of each other's concerns. It is because of these rare couples that I continue to have faith in the institution of marriage and of partnering. In my case, however, it was clear that nothing was going to change – my attempts at discussing the issues had not achieved any results. I began to realize that he was as unhappy here as I was thrilled to be experiencing my life's dream.

In retrospect, I think that what initially created the divergence of views was the fact that, while I had approached the Retreat as a project – a learning experience of sorts which would help me to reflect and apply in concrete terms my experiences of rural development over a 20-year period – Chez saw this merely as a business endeavour which was expected to yield profitable results! Thus, while I was perfectly contented with the fact that although there was no profit I was still able to provide employment, make my guests happy, apply my rural development principles and be happy in the process, he certainly was not contented. And perhaps understandably so, given that his experience and expectation had been, like most persons, that one embarks on a business enterprise for the purpose of generating profit! Clearly, for the sake of both parties, there had to be a parting of the ways, I thought, and, having taken that decision, my spirits rose – I felt a lightness of mind and body.

On suggesting finally to him (it took me several months to summon the courage!) that we bid each other a regretful farewell – with him taking his leave of the Retreat, leaving me to manage on my own – there was immediate acceptance, with little discussion, almost as if he were waiting all along for such a suggestion to be made. In August of 2004 he left, and I began to feel whole.

It was then that the unexpected happened. The business, which had not been exactly failing but merely limping along, immediately took a turn for the better. Doors on which I had been knocking now suddenly opened up and plans which had had to be put on hold could now be executed. Call it coincidence if you like but it was as if positive energy now began to emerge and make its presence felt in the day to day operations of the Retreat.

The Half-Miler Returns...

It was the summer of 2010 and I was in Boston, Massachusetts spending a few weeks with my daughter Lara and her family. She had married Kemo, a fellow student from the Gambia whom she had met at the Boston University School of Management. The wedding had taken place at the Retreat in 2000 and by the summer of 2010 they had had two daughters. An annual vacation with them was always a pleasant break and I would close the Retreat for the period that I would be away from Tobago.

As I sat one evening in their living room checking my email, to my great surprise and excitement there was one from Marina telling me that Earl Connell had been to Tobago on vacation and had called for me. Remember Earl, one of the boyfriends from my teenage years? I had not been in touch with him for about 50 years, ever since he left Trinidad. Sometimes I did wonder about him, where he was, what he had done with his life, whether he had continued with his athletic career (he ran a mean half mile and had won an athletic scholarship to a university in the US). I had even kept a couple of the gold medals he had given me. So many questions and no immediate answers. What made this communication even stranger was the fact that for that past year I had made several attempts to find out something about him through my friend Merle. She was in touch with one of his former associates at the track club to which he had belonged in Trinidad all those years ago, but the effort had drawn a blank. Her friend had no idea where Earl was or what he had done with his life in the interim.

I also found out from Marina that he currently lived in New Jersey and would be back there several days before I was scheduled to leave Boston. I emailed Marina right away, instructing her to ensure that he had Lara's phone number so that he could call me when he returned to New Jersey. Then I called Merle. "Remember I was looking for Earl?" I asked. "Well, *he* found *me*." When I told her what had transpired we couldn't stop laughing.

The wait for the phone call from Earl would not be long. In the daily conversations which followed that initial call we brought each other up to date with what had taken place in our respective lives. We had both married a couple of times, had a couple of children each. He had been in the military for a number of years and was currently a coach. Interestingly we were now both single – me for reasons with which the reader is familiar, in his case because he had lost his wife to cancer two years earlier.

The phone conversations became so regular that my daughter wanted to know whether I would be passing through New Jersey on my way back to Tobago. Of course, I wasn't. Why rush into anything? Back in Tobago, however, the phone calls seemed to increase in number and length. Hmmm.... Maybe there should indeed be a meeting? Christmas, perhaps? Why not? And so, the planning started. Well, to cut to the chase, Earl proposed marriage to me on the very day of his arrival and to my own surprise I accepted right away. Needless to say, everyone thought we were quite crazy, quite reckless and, as Lara put it, quite irresponsible.

What really do you know about this man, she wanted to know? How do you know that he has no ulterior motives? What about his background, his ability to support himself? Most importantly, she had not met him, had never heard about him before that fateful email, and had had no opportunity to "check him out"! She was fairly unforgiving and in the end, when I would not bow to her issues, she called Marina so that he could be checked out, by proxy, as it were.

The wedding took place in New Jersey in May of 2011, less than a year after the reunion. By then Lara had met Earl, taken to him and was my greatest source of support in planning the wedding. Her entire family participated – she was the matron of honour, her husband, Kemo, gave me away, and her two daughters, Khadijah and Regina (yes, Lara actually named both of her daughters after me – Khadijah's middle name is also Regina...) were flower girls. Even her month-old son, Sideeq also participated, looking resplendent in his white suit! Frank was also in attendance at the wedding with his new girlfriend. My friends from Bishop Anstey High School were there for me too – four of them attended the wedding as did two of Earl's friends from his former track club in Trinidad. Earl had received the approval of everyone.

Back in Tobago I was surprised to observe how well Earl fitted into his new context of nature, birds, rural living and the hospitality offered by Cuffie River. Realizing that he was ready and willing to be helpful with kitchen matters, I introduced him to table setting, dishwashing, juice making and shopping. It made and has continued to make life so much easier that I was able to accept more clientele than I would have done otherwise. We make a great kitchen team along with the other workers and find time to play what was his and now our favourite sport, table tennis, almost daily.

Not many years ago I was bemoaning the fact that my daughter was not interested in assuming the reins of the business and that maybe I would have to possibly depend on grandchildren to take it over one day. Now, the question does not even arise. Working in partnership with Earl I feel the energy, the joy of being able to live in what my guests call my own private paradise and I feel that we could go on forever. Beautiful and diversified as it is despite its small size, Tobago offers guests the opportunity to experience a variety of tours to waterfalls, reefs, wetlands, the oldest protected rainforest in the western hemisphere and, of course, beaches. The history of the island is as diversified as its physical offerings and so historical tours are offered. Most of our guests discover us via tour operators and popular websites, some of which list favourable comments from former guests. Most come from the United States and secondarily from Britain and the rest of Europe. The vast majority come to view the endemic species of birds we have, simply for pleasure or in some cases, professional photography. The 100 species or more that we have on the property include several different types of hummingbirds, with which I was not in the least familiar until the project was launched and they simply made their appearance. Nor have they left since.

Conclusion and Reflections

So, here I am, happy in my Tobago haven and with my decision to follow, in a sense, in my father's footsteps and to apply those principles introduced to me so many years ago in Geneva, Switzerland. To the responsibilities for operating the Retreat, I have added a short crop agricultural component to the tree cropping I had established at the beginning so that in between bird watching, guests can look forward to the meals which we try to make varied, wholesome, enjoyable and, most importantly, indigenous. Vegetables often come from my small kitchen garden where tomatoes, cabbage, cauliflower, broccoli, sweet and pimento peppers, cucumbers, ochroes, eggplant, beans and seasonings such as chives, thyme and basil are grown. Our tree crops include grapefruit, shaddock, lemons, limes, avocados, star fruit, pawpaw and tangerines. None of the juices served at the Retreat come out of a can or a box. They are all fresh and homemade.

Little by little I have become a small-time farmer, which has proven to be an absolutely fulfilling endeavour. The cocoa farmer's daughter has herself become a farmer in her own right. Nothing can really describe that feeling of swollen pride when one sees a seed which has been planted break the surface of the soil in the form of a tiny green shoot – a green shoot which in time and with care will yield a mass of produce intended for nourishing consumption. It really is a miracle of nature. The project has won several awards at the local, national and regional levels, among which have been some for environmental management and sustainable accommodation.

Sustainability and environmental management continue to be themes for which I have the greatest respect and which are practised consistently at the Retreat. When in 2009 the Commonwealth Heads of Government Meeting took place in Trinidad, it was attended by all but three member countries of the Commonwealth. The theme of the meeting, "Partnering for a More Equitable and Sustainable Future", laid the basis for the summit to address the threat of climate change – an issue which went to the heart of the concept of development as it began to take shape in my mind all those years ago in Geneva. What is ironical, however, is that while government and community leaders have now got into the habit of tossing around the various terms related to this issue and to describing it as a "defining" moment in history (or words to that effect), there is actually not much that they are doing to look the problem in the eye and deal with it, global socio-economic and health crises notwithstanding.

Renowned Caribbean economist Dr. Havelock Brewster, delivering his lecture on Caribbean development policy and regional community strategy at the UWI Distinguished Public Servants Lecture Series, June 1989, remarked: "It is a regrettable feature of life in this region that political leaders, whether they be of the political right, left or centre, conduct the business of government with an authoritarian disregard of the people they are supposed to serve. The opposition parties are no better." Decades later, Ambassador Brewster's comments unfortunately continue to ring true. It remains a source of amazement to rural development practitioners that in a region considered some 60% rural, scant effort is made at the formal level to meaningfully effect transformation of the rural sector via an integrated and consistent strategy of support and programming. Successive governments make clear their position with regard to the development of what are considered key pillars of the economy – agriculture, manufacturing, agro-industry, tourism, fishing. Rarely, however, is more than lip service paid to rural development as an integrated sector, combining components of production, marketing, health, education (formal and non-formal), infrastructure, environmental management, communications and recreation.

But how best are we to respond to the needs of our communities? How best to fulfill those responsibilities required to ensure that true development occurs in our various countries? And, if by "we" is meant not simply central governments and other officials and relevant authorities, but also communities and the families within those communities, then there must be put in place systems to ensure that true development principles apply. Central to the approach is the issue of people and their well-being – physical, mental, intellectual.

This said, there is much that grassroots communities themselves, particularly in the rural sectors, can do. Take, for example, the question of fruit and vegetables produced in rural areas mainly. Quite often, such produce can be utilized in myriad ways: fruit too ripe to be eaten can be blended for use in juices, breads and cakes while vegetables that have passed their prime can be made into soups. An excess in the production of both fruit and vegetables can be handled via freezing and storing for use at a later stage. Domestic animals, poultry and wildlife should also be beneficiaries of produce not suitable for human consumption, but which could be put to use in this regard. In short, everything produced on the land should be absorbed in some way or other for the welfare of the family, the community and the nation at large.

Greater advantage can be taken of sun and wind power as substitutes for man-made energy. I don't think we realize how powerful the sun's rays can be in the destruction of bacteria. Further, the choices we make in the purchase of items for consumption go a long way in determining the role we play in the process of climate change and global warming. Do we consider the biodegradable nature of the packaging? And how do we dispose of this packaging? Do we buy cans when boxes will suffice? Foil wrapping paper as against regular paper? The truth of the matter is that consumer choices can do a lot to dictate the ways in which manufacturers and industrialists package and present their goods. But there has to be awareness and sensitivity. We must build a consciousness which becomes like second nature, with each person doing his or her part to protect the environment while responding to issues arising from climate change and global warming, and preserving human dignity.

As for me, I have tried to be proactive. I have determined my priorities and executed them to the best of my ability. But I have enjoyed a great deal of good luck as well, a factor often overlooked by persons in determining why they have been fortunate in the achievement of their life goals. There have been challenges, yes, but I have never sunk to the depths of despair, never experienced any life-threatening illness, or extreme loss in my life. I have conquered the challenges, such as they were, via a strong will to move forward, hard work and creativity. But maybe here again it was the spirit and example of Adeline that prevailed.

What I have discovered is that being happy is the ultimate goal of one's life and that this comes from a mindset of peace, of contentment and the wisdom to utilize to the fullest the abilities with which we were born and or which we have the potential to develop. When I count myself as "happy" it encompasses this reality, but more so the recognition of the gifts that money cannot buy – in my case, great friendships and loving and supportive family members among whom are six healthy grandchildren and a great granddaughter, Skylar. Could one ask for more? Frank Ayodele granted me Tineisha, Ayola and Zharia; and Janine Omolara gave me Khadijah, Regina and my only grandson, Sideeq. Skylar is the product of first grandchild, Tineisha.

For the second time in my life, my cup runneth over....

At the Retreat with my Japanese guest, Midori Sato – stellar wildlife photographer!
(photo courtesy of Mr. Sato)

*4-year-old great grand-
daughter Skylar*

*7-year-old grandson Sideeq's reac-
tion – "YaY!" – on hearing that he
is mentioned in the* MEMOIR

Glimpses of Cuffie River Nature Retreat ➢

Pages 162-164 Photos reproduced by courtesy of:
Faraaz Abdool (5,11,16,17), Gerry Flemming (3,7,9,10,12)
Roger Neckles (20), Brigitte Noel (6,8,18)
Steve Wooler (1,2,4,13,14,15,19,21)

🌿 Epilogue

ADELINE DIED IN July of 1998, the same year I began the operation of the Retreat and just over a month before she would have
turned 96. In a joint tribute to our mother, Reggie, Marina and I
reflected on the many things she had taught us by example – respect
for self and others, support for those in need, manifestation of
honour and strength in the way one lives. In short, we recognized
that one of the greatest lessons was to treat others the way we
wished to be treated ourselves. We acknowledged that through
teaching, supporting and comforting us – albeit in a no-nonsense
kind of way – she had created a safety net of love, knowing that if
life ever knocked us down she would be there to lift us up. Not that
she would ever have to, since those lessons of strength were not
only well taught, but also well practised by her children.

To exhibit what a pillar of strength she represented for me, I
remember in my early teenage years, waiting up for her to get home
after she journeyed to Chaguanas to collect the monthly rents from
the properties that Reginald had left her. Chaguanas seemed a long
way from Tunapuna in those days and as I sat alone waiting for
her, I would wonder what I would ever do if she never came home.
Suppose there was an accident that took her life? I would try, but
simply could not begin to fathom what life for me could possibly
be like without my mother, my siblings notwithstanding. Then,
without fail, I would finally hear the squeak of the gate and jump up
from the rocking chair in which I had been sitting, bemoaning a fate
that was not to be – at least for now. I would welcome my mother
with joy and relief, but without sharing with her or anyone else, my
prior broodings. And this joy and relief knew no bounds when she
finally sold those houses and bought the Park Lane property where
I spent the rest of my adolescent years until I married Frank and
moved away. When I reflect on it, I realize that her presence was so
dominating, so all-encompassing that simply to know that she was
there was enough for me. I desired almost nothing more except that
my father were alive, to talk to me, to hear my complaints against

the very one I could not do without – Adeline; to put my arms around his neck and have him cuddle me, an experience I had never had since he had been too weak, according to Adeline, to hold me even as a newborn baby....

The degenerative and disastrous Alzheimer's disease which threw the fatal curve ball that would eventually be responsible for the final breath drawn by Adeline, had in fact, at least two years earlier, taken its toll. She had lived and drawn breath for these two years, but the spirit which had represented the being we knew had withdrawn from her physical body. What was amazing, however, was that her essence – that which intrinsically defined her and who she was – remained up to the time of her death and beyond. My siblings and I have all continued on our respective journeys on our own but secure in the reality of her spirit accompanying us every step of the way. I don't think of her as deceased. I simply think of her, as I do of my father... much of the time.

Abbreviations & Acronyms

ART • Agency for Rural Transformation

BIMAP • Barbados Institute of Management and Productivity

CADEC • Christian Action for Development in the Caribbean

CAFRA • Caribbean Association for Feminist Research and Action

CARDI • Caribbean Agricultural Regional Development Institute

CARICOM • Caribbean Community

CARIPEDA • Caribbean People's Development Agency

CCA • Caribbean Conservation Association

CCC • Caribbean Conference of Churches

CCPD • Commission for the Churches' Participation in Development

CNIRD • Caribbean Network for Integrated Rural Development

CPDC • Caribbean Policy Development Centre

CUSO • Canadian University Services Overseas (*now* CUSO International)

DFC • Development Fund Committee

ECLAC • United Nations Economic Commission for Latin America and the Caribbean

EEC • European Economic Community

FAO • Food and Agricultural Organization

GFC • Grenada Farms Corporation

GNP • Grenada National Party

GULP • Grenada United Labour Party

ICTA • Imperial College of Tropical Agriculture

IICA • Inter-American Institute for Cooperation in Agriculture

INCARD • Information Network for Caribbean Rural Development

ISER • Institute of Social and Economic Research (*now* SALISES • Sir Arthur Lewis Institute of Social and Economic Studies)

LDA • Local Development Agency

LIAT • Leeward Islands Air Transport

MNIB • Marketing and National Import Board

NACDA • National Cooperative Development Agency

NGO • non-governmental organization

NJAC • National Joint Action Committee

NJM • New Jewel Movement

OAS • Organization of American States

OECS • Organization of Eastern Caribbean States

PDP • Projects Development Programme

PFU • Productive Farmers' Union

- Abbreviations & Acronyms

PRA • People's Revolutionary Army
PRG • People's Revolutionary Government
RMC • Revolutionary Military Council
UCWI • University College of the West Indies
WCC • World Council of Churches
WINFA • Windward Islands Farmers' Association